S0-ASB-668

THE 20 MINUTE COOK BOOK

Michael Reise

CROWN PUBLISHERS, INC.
NEW YORK

LIBRARY OF CONGRESS CATALOG CARD NUMBER: 53-5249

Printed in the United States of America
American Book–Stratford Press, Inc., New York

For Dorothy

with gratitude for her good taste

and good appetite

ACKNOWLEDGMENTS

My deep and special thanks go to my wife, for priceless help on this entire project; to my mother, for the influence of her unforgettably good cooking; to Cecelia Bellm and Dorothy Martin, for knowing comment and criticism of the original manuscript, to Justin Greene for steady encouragement.

Contents

Introduction

Cooks of the old school, and maybe even you yourself, were trained to believe that the only way to prepare really *good* food was the hard way: starting from scratch with raw ingredients, and putting in whatever hours of kitchen time were needed.

Today you're demanding more and more ready-prepared foods —"something quick, easy, and good"—and there's a very good reason why.

You've discovered that despite your streamlined kitchen, cookery's peeling and boiling is just plain drudgery; you've found out that you're actually a prisoner in your house while a baking process goes on; you've realized that it takes no cooking skill at all, and a good deal of your precious time, to measure and sift and measure and sift again.

Accordingly, you've made your complaints good and loud—and that's why you can now buy almost every food known to man, in one or another prepared form—with a good part of the drudgery-work done.

Some viewers-with-alarm would have you think that this flood of packaged foods hints at an eventual disappearance of the art of fine cooking.

Don't you believe it—not for a minute!

What always has and always will count in cooking is *what you serve and how it tastes,* not how much hard labor you've put into its preparation.

If your food is easy to make, good! If it's as easy as opening a package and adding some of your magic touches, *so much the better!*

So use packaged foods and use them often. If there are varieties you haven't yet sampled, try them. There are plenty to choose from —and the packages carry brand names which are among America's finest. That means you can always depend on purity, quality, and plenty for your money!

There are three types of packaged foods:

READY TO COOK (such as frozen vegetables)

READY TO EAT (such as canned vegetables, meats, fish, or fruit)
READY MIXED (such as biscuit or pancake mix)

Packaged food cookery is virtually foolproof. You can count on good results. You merely follow recipes and are reasonably accurate about measurements, time, and temperature.

Do packaged foods *really* save work? Here's a side-by-side picture of biscuits made the old way and the biscuit-mix way:

OLD WAY	BISCUIT-MIX WAY
1. Get out the flour bag	1. Get out the biscuit mix
2. Get out the shortening	2. Get out the salt
3. Get out the baking powder	3. Get out the sugar
4. Get out the salt	4. Get out the milk
5. Get out the milk	5. Get out the measuring cup
6. Get out the flour sifter	6. Get out the measuring spoons
7. Get out a measuring cup	7. Get out a bowl
8. Get out the measuring spoons	8. Measure biscuit mix into bowl
9. Get out some waxed paper	9. Return biscuit mix to shelf
10. Get out a mixing bowl	10. Measure and add salt to mix
11. Put flour into sifter	11. Return salt to shelf
12. Sift flour onto waxed paper	12. Measure and add sugar to mix
13. Measure out flour needed	13. Return sugar to shelf
14. Return excess flour to bag	14. Measure and add milk—
15. Return flour bag to shelf	
16. Measure and add salt	
17. Return salt to shelf	
18. Measure and add baking powder	
19. Return baking powder to shelf	
20. Put flour, baking powder and salt into sifter	
21. Sift	
22. Put flour, baking powder and salt into sifter *again*	
23. Sift again	
24. Return sifter to cupboard—	

—But why go on? Here you are barely started, the old way—and practically finished, the *new* way. So you answer the question for yourself: do packaged mixes save time?

And biscuits aren't just an isolated example. The same pattern of work *saved* repeats itself with every packaged food you use.

In an old-fashioned recipe, *you* do the work. Using packaged foods, the work is done for you.

Notes, Thoughts, and Hints

MAKE YOUR OWN "MIXES"

Keep on hand ready-mixed supplies of mixtures you constantly use, bread crumbs and grated cheese, for example.

You can even combine the dry ingredients of your own recipes for biscuits, muffins, cakes, cookies, pancakes, etc., and store them in large glass jars. A little arithmetic will quickly give you the proportions of liquid and shortening ingredients to use for each batch of your own mix.

READ AND *RE-READ* THE RECIPE

Take a few extra seconds to study the recipe you're starting, and you'll be paid back in minutes saved. The more familiar you are with the directions, the easier it is to cook—and you won't have to stop operations constantly to consult your cook book.

TIMESAVING COOKING METHODS

Follow our directions for *method* as well as ingredients. Recipes have been worked out so that you waste no time waiting for part of a dish to cook before proceeding with the next step.

"ONE-DISH MEALS"

—The timesavingest of all timesavers. They contain the "meat," potatoes and vegetables all in one—and need only a hot bread and a green salad as go-withs. Don't underestimate the importance of hot bread and salad; these add not only bulk and goodness to the meal, but plenty of color and interest.

SEASON WITH A LIGHT TOUCH

Remember that prepared foods are already seasoned by the

packer. All you need do is perk up the flavor a little. So be careful when adding seasonings—it's easy to overdo it.

SEASONINGS AND SEASONING INGREDIENTS

Salt: Salt should be added only until you can taste the full flavor of the food. Test as you go; packaged foods vary greatly in the amount of salt needed.

Pepper: If possible, buy a pepper mill and grind your own; there's an unbelievable difference in flavoring power. But if you prefer to use ready-ground pepper, buy good brands which you know are pure, and buy small quantities, often.

Celery Salt: Use it with a free hand in meat, fish, fowl, or salads. But remember that celery salt *is* salt. Where only a little *salt* is needed, use celery salt instead.

Onion Juice: A little adds a lot of flavor and brings out richness. Like all bottled sauces, the potency of onion juice varies from brand to brand. This book uses a medium-strength juice. Find the brand you like and stay with it.

Garlic: Use it sparingly and garlic rewards you with real flavor. You never have to worry about detecting it, either in the food or on the breath, if you keep a light touch.

Herbs: Use them often. You need no specialized knowledge of cooking, nor do you need a large collection. (See Index for more about herbs.)

Soy Sauce: An excellent seasoner for any food containing mushrooms; it heightens their flavor.

Other Sauces: Worcestershire or similar sauces add flavor to soups, stews, and chowders. Be sparing, however, unless you want the taste of the sauce to predominate.

Sour Cream: One of the best enrichments you can use. You can't taste it because it blends right in with the other flavors.

Timesaving Utensil Hints

POT SETS OR POT SENSE?

Graduated sets of pots and pans look mighty pretty hanging on your kitchen wall, but how many times have you had to wash and rewash that single small saucepan in the course of cooking a meal? Moral: buy two or three or more, each, of the pans you most often use, and save a lot of cooking time.

"HOUSECLEAN" THE POT CUPBOARD

Just because you have a collection of old-fashioned pots and pans that belonged to Grandma is no reason for *you* to keep on using them. If you're sentimental, put them away in a safe place where they won't wear out—and buy yourself shiny new replacements. You'll be amazed at the time and work efficient pots and pans can save.

IT'S YOUR MONEY — BUY THE BEST UTENSILS

Fine quality pots and pans should last for years, so buy the best you can get. You'll be repaid many times over in the satisfaction and ease of cooking with good utensils.

SOME HANDY KITCHEN TOOLS TO HAVE

A French cook's whisk — nothing better or faster for making smooth sauces, combining liquid ingredients, or beating thin mixtures.

Two sets of measuring spoons, so you don't have to take time to wash and dry spoons used for measuring liquids, when you want to measure *dry* ingredients.

Two sets of ¼- ⅓- and ½-cup measuring cups, for the same reason as two sets of measuring spoons.

Three pyrex measuring cups—quart (4-cup), pint (2-cup) and 1-cup size. The larger-size cups very often double for mixing bowls and save much time when adding one liquid to another to make up a total quantity of more than 1 cup.

A kitchen timing clock that accurately measures down to one minute. The best we've found for the purpose is a photographer's darkroom clock that sounds an alarm when the time is up.

The best kitchen knives money can buy. Nothing eats up kitchen time and makes cooking hard work more than dull knives. *Good* knives hold their edges indefinitely. Never use a plastic or metal knife holder; and don't cram knives into a drawer. Buy a wooden holder and your knives will stay sharp.

Cheap pie tins to line with aluminum foil, for broiling or oven heating. Save scouring burned-on grease from your good pans.

A small strainer makes a very handy sifter for small quantities of flour, sugar, cocoa, etc. Keep one especially for this purpose.

A nutmeg grater, for making tablespoon-lots of bread crumbs or grated cheese.

Extra ice cube trays so you won't have to empty your regular trays when you want to chill foods quickly.

A portable electric mixer, even if you already own a big mixer. Place it so that it's right over your work surface, and arrange to keep it always plugged-in, ready to use when you pick it up.

KEEP YOUR TOOLS HANDY

Take a tip from Father's cellar workshop, and hang *your* tools up on the wall over your working surface—yes, can opener, mixing spoons, measuring cups, whisk, rotary beater, and all the rest.

Tools crowded into a drawer are not only hard to locate, but the constant shuffling helps wear them out.

Serving Hints

MENU MAKING

Keep your menus simple so that your *fancy* cooking isn't overshadowed. If the main dish is elaborate, serve a simple broth or consommé for soup and a fruit dessert. If the main dish includes rice or other starchy food, omit potatoes; serve a green vegetable or two.

Don't forget that hot bread and salad add a bountiful touch to any meal.

Pace dessert to the meal: serve fruit after heavy main dishes; fancier or more filling desserts after simple meals.

Look for ONE-DISH meals scattered through the main course chapters; in a very few minutes after you've put on your apron (or your chef's hat!) you can put a complete and delicious meal on the table that looks, tastes, and satisfies as though you'd gone to considerable time and trouble in the preparation.

If you haven't introduced "Soup Suppers" to your family, try it. Make the soup thick and hearty; serve plenty of it; add a hot bread, salad, and a whipped cream dessert. You'll please even "meat n' potatoes" people.

MENU "TIMING"

"Time to make" on our recipes includes *all the preparation and cooking time.* Check your recipe: in many cases you spend only a few minutes actually *working* on a dish; during the remainder of the time called for, you need only take an occasional peek to see what's going on in the pot (half the fun of cooking!). Choose what you're going to serve according to how much of your attention is required by the main dish. If little is needed, then make more elaborate side dishes or dessert.

"ALWAYS LEAVE THEM LAUGHING"

That's a cardinal rule of show business. It says, in effect: make your exit on a peak, before your audience tires.

The same rule applies to food. Naturally, don't allow people to leave your table hungry, but keep in mind that big portions of rich food tend to cloy the taste, and diminish the enjoyment of the meal.

Fill the "gaps" with salad or hot breads or other complementary culinary delights—you'll be a much better cook and host for it!

WINES

There's no trick to selecting wines to serve with meals: just be sure to buy *good* wine (there are many delicious domestic wines on the market), and for *food* accompaniment, dry (not sweet) wine.

The best varieties of dry white wines are Chablis, Sauterne, Graves, or Moselle. Among the red wines choose Burgundy or Claret.

The choice of red or white wine is up to your individual taste, although the lighter white wines generally go best with fish, fowl, or salads; the more robust red wines, with heavier meat dishes, or hearty soups.

Whether or not to cool the wine is again a matter of your personal taste. If you do cool it, don't *chill* it.

DON'T FORGET THE GARNISH

Food should both *taste* and *look* as if it has been made with lavish care. That's where garnishes help. Use them often, as the recipes suggest.

IS COMPANY COMING?

To be cool and unflustered while making a meal for company; to serve the hot food *hot* and the chilled food *cold*—and in general to insure a good time for *yourself* as well as your guests, make a time schedule for the cooking of the entire meal well ahead of time.

Write down every step of the entire preparation, allowing yourself ample time to do what's necessary. Add up how much time you've allotted, count back from when you want to serve, and you'll know when to start cooking.

Just by the way, warn your guests in advance that you expect them to be prompt. Then give or take a few minutes, but when dinner is ready, serve it!

WHAT TO MAKE FOR DINNER?

Cooking often becomes half knowing how, and half knowing *what* to cook. Spend an occasional few minutes leafing through your cook book, making notes on the inside back cover of recipes you mean to try "when you get a chance." Your chance comes when you're stuck for what-to-make.

SPEAKING OF LEAFING THROUGH A COOK BOOK—

Leaf through *this* one, looking for the TIMESAVERS. You'll find many hints for short-cutting food preparation.

AND JUST A FINAL WORD—

The recipes in this book were developed, tested, and timed in a postage-stamp-size apartment kitchenette, using the everyday utensils found in any kitchen.

Soup

Easy, Thrifty, and Good

Thick, hearty soup, served with a hot bread, plus a simple salad and a good dessert, makes a substantial meal. Add a bottle of wine, and you have company fare!

ENHANCING CANNED CREAM-STYLE SOUPS

Hints

Where package directions call for liquid to be added, use milk, or half milk and half light cream; for a heartier soup, use ⅔ milk and ⅓ clear chicken broth.

Add less liquid than package directions call for, to intensify the flavor.

Add a good shake of celery salt, a pinch of sugar, and a liberal chunk of butter. Stir well, and serve.

Add about ½ cup of the cooked vegetable: for example, green peas to cream of pea soup.

While heating soup, add a small onion, cut in half. Discard before serving.

To cream of tomato soup add ½ cup tomato juice as part of the liquid, plus a dash of Worcestershire sauce.

Two tablespoons of sour cream stirred through cream soups just before serving work wonders.

Just before serving cream of celery soup add 4 to 6 tablespoons finely chopped celery (see Timesaver Index for a quick way to chop it). Float a crisp leaf or two from the celery heart on each portion.

Float one tablespoon slightly salted whipped cream on each portion of cream soup. Sprinkle with a few grains of paprika.

Always try to serve croutons or a garnish with cream soups. For quick and easy hints see end of this chapter.

Most cream soups take well to a sprinkling of blanched almonds, lightly toasted in butter, then salted. Make these yourself, or keep a can on hand.

Creamed soups look exciting with thin slices of cucumber floating on top. (See Index for Fancy Cucumber Service.)

Sprinkle creamed soups with dry "popcorn" style cheese, very lightly salted.

Hints

ENHANCING CANNED "HEARTY"-STYLE SOUPS

Use tomato juice as part of the liquid to be added to meat or vegetable soups.

Reduce liquid amount called for to intensify the flavor.

Add a bay leaf tip and a few celery leaves while heating. Discard before serving.

Add a small onion, cut in half, while heating. Discard before serving; or sauté onion, finely chopped, in 1 tablespoon butter until soft and yellow (3 or 4 minutes), using your soup kettle. Add soup, and heat as usual.

Rub an area about 2 inches square on the bottom of your soup kettle with a cut clove of garlic, before starting soup.

Cooked vegetables, especially leftovers such as cut

corn, peas, lima beans, snap beans, or carrots, may be added for additional flavor. If soup is too thick, add chicken broth as needed.

Frozen mixed vegetables may be cooked right in the soup while it is heating. Use ½ package to 2 cans of soup. Taste and correct seasoning before serving.

Crackers or croutons add interest to canned stock soups, and serve nicely to stretch a small quantity. For quick and easy crouton hints see end of this chapter.

MAKE YOUR *OWN* SOUP THIS EASY WAY

Hint

Much of the work that goes into soup is in preparing the stock. Use prepared stock as a base and save much time and effort. Basic stock ingredients can be stored indefinitely on your kitchen shelf, except for bouillon cubes. Buy these often, in small quantities; keep in a tightly closed container.

SOUP STOCK—CHICKEN I

Use canned plain chicken broth without dilution, or dilute concentrated liquid broth with slightly less water than called for.

SOUP STOCK—CHICKEN II

Use dehydrated "chicken soup," the kind available in small foil envelopes. May be used as is for a soup base with ½ cup less water than called for on package. Or, for clear stock, strain the soup; save the strainings for another dish.

SOUP STOCK—VEGETABLE

Use dehydrated "vegetable" or "vegetable-tomato" soup, the kind available in small foil envelopes. May be used as is for a soup base with ½ cup less water than called for on package. Or, for clear stock, strain the soup; save the strainings for another dish.

SOUP STOCK—BOUILLON TYPE

Use bouillon cubes, beef extract, or soup powders (the kind packed in small cellophane envelopes). These products vary in taste from brand to brand—experiment to find the flavor you like and then stay with that brand.

Consommé may also be used; however, your finished soup will have some of the characteristic flavor of consommé.

For the "clearest" flavor, in which the stock does not overpower the taste of the basic ingredient in the soup, use chicken stock.

10 to 12 min.

BEAN SOUP

1 cup chicken stock
1½ cups water
2 thin slices boiled ham
2 cans condensed bean soup
1 cup cooked carrots (optional)
½ teaspoon onion juice
1 teaspoon dried celery flakes
salt and pepper

Bring stock and water to a boil over high heat. Meanwhile, dice ham, open soup, drain and rinse carrots if canned. Add all to boiling stock mixture, with onion juice and celery flakes. Mix well, taste and correct seasoning, simmer over low heat for a few minutes before serving.

Serves 4 generously

BEAN SOUP—VARIATIONS

MACARONI: Add ½ cup or more (dry measure) macaroni, cooked until tender in lightly salted water.

TOMATO: Add 1 or more fresh tomatoes, chopped, or up to 1 cup canned whole-pack tomatoes, broken into coarse chunks.

BACON: Just before serving, sprinkle crumbled crisp bacon over each portion, or, brown chopped bacon in soup pot and drain off fat before starting to cook soup.

VEGETABLE BEAN SOUP

water
1 envelope dehydrated vegetable soup
2 tablespoons butter
1 onion, chopped fine
1 #2 can cooked dried lima beans
1 teaspoon dehydrated parsley
salt and pepper

Measure ½ cup less water than called for on soup package into saucepan and start boiling over highest heat. In soup pot melt butter, add onion and cook 3 to 5 minutes over medium heat, or until soft and yellow. Add all other ingredients and boiling water. Bring to a boil over high heat; reduce heat and simmer 10 minutes. Just before serving taste and correct seasoning with salt and pepper.

20 min.

Serves 4 generously

BEAN AND MACARONI SOUP

3 cups water
1 8-oz. package macaroni and cheese dinner
2 cups chicken broth
1 package frozen mixed vegetables
1 fresh tomato sliced, or 1 cup canned tomatoes
1 #2 can cooked dried lima beans
salt and pepper

20 min.

Lightly salt water. Bring to a boil over highest heat, add half the macaroni; reserve remainder for another dish. Cook for time directed on package and drain. Meanwhile, bring chicken broth to a boil, add frozen vegetables and tomato. Cook as directed on vegetable package; when tender, add macaroni and beans; combine; taste and correct seasoning with salt and pepper. Simmer 5 minutes; sprinkle each portion with grated cheese from macaroni dinner.

Serves 4 to 6

15 min.

BEET SOUP, COLD (BORSCHT)

1 #2 can diced beets, chilled
1 8-oz. jar "junior" beets, chilled
cold water
2 egg yolks
2 tablespoons lemon juice
2 teaspoons sugar
½ teaspoon salt
¼ teaspoon ground ginger, or less
1 pint sour cream

Strain liquid from beets into a measuring cup, add water to make 1 cup and pour into a deep mixing bowl. Add 2 cups water and egg yolks; beat briskly with a rotary beater. Add all other ingredients, reserving half the sour cream, and beat again. Add all the beets, stir, taste and correct seasoning. The soup may need a bit more sugar. Serve in deep bowls with a generous gob of sour cream in each.

Note: For richer borscht, use ½ cup clear chicken broth instead of ½ cup water.

Serves 4

Hint

BORSCHT "SUPPER"

For a light, delicious summer supper, serve a hot boiled baby potato or two (see Index for Canned Boiled Potatoes) in each bowl of borscht. To your meal add a green salad, a brown-and-serve hot bread, a bottle of cooled white wine and a whipped cream dessert. You'll earn cheers!

CHOWDER SOUP BASE

3 cups milk or 2 cups milk and 1 cup light cream
½ cup chicken broth
1 #2 can boiled baby potatoes
1 cup kernel-style corn, canned or cooked
1 teaspoon dehydrated onion flakes
½ teaspoon Worcestershire sauce
tiny pinch of nutmeg
pinch of thyme
¼ teaspoon salt
dusting of pepper

10 to 12 min.

Measure milk or milk and cream into a saucepan and place over medium heat to pre-heat. Measure chicken broth into soup pot, add all other ingredients (drain and rinse canned vegetables). Place over medium heat, add pre-heated milk and cream. Simmer 5 minutes. Taste and correct seasoning with salt and pepper.

Serves 4 generously

FISH CHOWDER

20 min.

Prepare Chowder Soup Base (see above). While simmering, cut 1 pound frozen-thawed or fresh flounder or cod filets into chunks or 1 inch cubes. Add to base as soon as fish is cut; start counting cooking time and simmer 8 to 15 minutes, depending on thickness of fish, or until fish flakes when tested with a fork.

CRAB OR LOBSTER CHOWDER

18 min.

Prepare Chowder Soup Base (see above). While simmering, pick over 1 pound or less fresh-cooked crab or lobster meat, or use well-drained canned. When base has simmered for the 5 minutes directed, add shellfish and simmer 5 to 8 minutes more.

18 min.

SHRIMP CHOWDER

Prepare Chowder Soup Base (see above). When ready, add 1 to 2 cups cooked, shelled, and deveined shrimp. Fresh, frozen-thawed, or canned may be used. Simmer 5 to 8 minutes and serve.

18 min.

CLAM CHOWDER

Prepare Chowder Soup Base (see above). When ready, add 1 12-oz. can chopped clams, drained, and simmer 5 to 8 minutes.

20 min.

CLAM CHOWDER, MANHATTAN STYLE

½ cup tomato juice
1 cup bottled or canned clam juice
1 cup water
a generous pinch of thyme
1 12-oz. can chopped clams
1 can condensed clam chowder
1 can condensed vegetable soup, vegetarian style
1 tablespoon butter
salt, pepper, celery salt

Start boiling, over highest heat, tomato juice, clam juice, water, and thyme. Add clams, well drained, clam chowder, vegetable soup and butter. Reduce heat and simmer 12 to 15 minutes. Before serving, taste and correct seasoning with salt, pepper, and celery salt, adding a little more thyme if desired.

Serves 4 to 6

20 min.

CORN CHOWDER

½ cup chicken broth
½ package frozen cut corn
1 12-oz. can Vichysoisse soup
1 soup can of milk
butter
a tiny pinch of thyme
salt and pepper

Bring broth to a boil over highest heat, add corn, reduce heat, and cook corn for time directed on package. Meanwhile, in another pan heat soup combined with milk. Add corn and broth when ready. Mix well, add a generous chunk of butter and pinch of thyme. Taste and correct seasoning with salt and pepper; simmer 5 minutes.

For a slightly thicker soup, stir 2 teaspoons flour until smooth with ½ cup of the soup liquid; add to soup with butter and thyme.

Note: If desired, 1 cup or more canned boiled baby potatoes, drained and rinsed, may be added with cooked corn.

Serves 4 generously

INTO THE SOUP POT WITH LEFTOVERS

Hint

Small amounts of leftover vegetables or casserole dishes can go right into the chowder or soup pot. Leftover macaroni-and-cheese, for example, added to vegetable soup gives you a miniature minestrone-style soup.

LENTIL SOUP

15 min.

- 2 cans condensed lentil soup
- 1 cup chicken stock
- 1½ cups water
- 2 strips raw bacon, diced
- 1 small onion, chopped
- salt and pepper
- sour cream

Combine soup, stock and water in a saucepan and place over medium heat to pre-heat. In soup pot fry bacon until brown, add onion, cook 2 or 3 minutes; drain off fat. Add soup, and mix. Taste and correct seasoning with salt and pepper. Simmer 7 to 10 minutes and serve, with a spoonful of sour cream in each portion, if desired.

Serves 4 generously

LENTIL SOUP—VARIATIONS

POTATO: Add diced freshly boiled potatoes to soup just before serving, or use canned boiled baby potatoes, drained, rinsed, and heated in boiling water.

FRANKFURTER: Omit bacon. Slice 1 or 2 frankfurters into thin rounds and add to soup with chicken stock.

Timesaver: Use miniature or cocktail frankfurters or Vienna sausages, instead of regular frankfurters. Drain off liquid and add to soup whole.

MUSHROOM: Add one or two 3-oz. cans mushroom caps and liquid with chicken stock.

up to 20 min.

CONSOMMÉ MADRILENE

Ask your grocer for chilled consommé. (If you buy in a self-service store, reach into the back or bottom of cooler where the soup will be best chilled.) If not available chilled, turn soup into an ice cube tray and place in freezing compartment of refrigerator. Stir occasionally. It should be firm enough to serve in 15 to 18 minutes. To serve: sprinkle a few grains of curry powder over each portion of chilled soup, or stir ⅛ teaspoon curry into soup before chilling. Garnish with lemon wedges or push a stalk or two of heart-of-celery into each portion.

12-oz. can serves 3 or 4

15 min.

MUSHROOM SOUP

2 cans condensed cream of mushroom soup
1 cup milk
½ cup chicken broth
1 cup water
1 tablespoon butter
1 3-oz. can mushrooms
1 teaspoon soy sauce
salt and pepper

Combine soup, milk, broth and water in a saucepan; place over medium heat to pre-heat. In soup pot melt butter, add mushrooms and soy sauce; simmer over low heat 3 or 4 minutes. Add soup; simmer 10 minutes. Taste and correct seasoning with salt and pepper.

Note: If available in your locality, add buckwheat groats to soup just before serving. Prepare as directed on package, allowing about ¼ cup cooked groats for each serving.

Serves 4 generously

PEA SOUP

- 2 cans condensed pea soup
- 8 canned pork sausages
- 1 cup chicken stock
- 1½ cups water
- ¼ teaspoon onion juice
- a tiny pinch of ground cloves
- ½ cup cooked carrots, for color
- salt and pepper

12 to 15 min.

Combine all ingredients except sausages and seasonings and place over medium heat. Arrange sausages in a foil-lined pie tin and brown as directed on can under broiler. When soup is heated through, taste and correct seasoning with salt and pepper. When sausages are ready, cut into thick slices (allow 2 sausages to a portion) and place in soup bowls; pour soup over.

Serves 4 generously

PEA SOUP—VARIATIONS

HAM: Omit sausages. Add up to 1 cup lean boiled ham, chopped coarsely, just before serving.

BACON: Omit sausages. Just before serving, sprinkle crumbled crisp bacon over each portion, or brown a few strips of bacon, chopped, in soup pot and drain off fat before starting to cook soup.

FRANKFURTER: Omit sausages. Slice 1 or 2 frankfurters into thin rounds and add to soup with chicken stock.

Timesaver: Use miniature or cocktail frankfurters or Vienna sausages, instead of regular frankfurters. Drain off liquid and add to soup whole.

POTATO SOUP

20 min.

- 2 cups milk
- ½ cup water
- 2 tablespoons butter
- 1 small onion, chopped
- 1 #2 can boiled baby potatoes
- ½ can condensed cream of celery soup
- parsley
- salt and pepper
- celery salt

Combine milk and water in a saucepan and place over medium heat to pre-heat. Melt butter in soup pot over medium high heat; add onion and cook 4 minutes or until onion browns slightly. Drain and rinse potatoes; crush about half of them with a fork. Add pre-heated milk, soup, potatoes and 1 teaspoon parsley to onions; simmer 8 to 10 minutes. Taste and correct seasoning with salt, pepper, and celery salt before serving.

Serves 4 generously

POTATO SOUP—VARIATIONS

MUSHROOM: Add one 3-oz. can button mushrooms to soup when adding potatoes.

HAM: Just before serving, add ¼ pound or more sliced boiled ham, diced.

BUCKWHEAT GROATS: If this cereal is available in your locality, cook as directed on package, allowing about ¼ cup for each portion. Add to finished soup.

POTATO SOUP GARNISH

15 min.

Toast rye bread crisply; butter generously, and float several inch-squares on each portion. So much the better if you can get heavy black pumpernickel.

VICHYSOISSE

To serve hot: Heat ½ cup chicken broth to boiling. Add a 12-oz. can of Vichysoisse, mix, and simmer 10 minutes on low heat. Taste and correct seasoning with salt and pepper; a dash of celery salt helps, too. Stir in a small chunk of butter and serve garnished with parsley.

5 min.

To serve cold: Have soup chilled in refrigerator (many stores sell it ready-chilled during the hot summer months). Whip ⅓ cup heavy cream, adding ⅛ teaspoon salt. Turn soup into a deep bowl and beat with a rotary beater until smooth. Taste and correct seasoning with salt, pepper, and celery salt. Fold in whipped cream and serve garnished with chopped parsley.

Note: For thinner soup, add ⅓ cup milk before folding in cream.

One 12-oz. can serves 2

TOMATO BOUILLON

15 min.

- 1½ cups tomato juice
- ¼ cup water
- 1 beef bouillon cube or more (beef extract may be used)
- 1 teaspoon dehydrated celery flakes
- salt and pepper

Bring all ingredients to a boil and simmer 10 minutes. Taste and correct seasoning with salt and pepper before serving.

Serves 2

10 min.

SUMMER SOUP (TOMATO)

2 cans condensed tomato soup, well chilled
½ cup heavy cream
salt
½ cup milk
1 tablespoon dry sherry wine
ice cubes
croutons or soup garnish

If soup is not chilled, turn it into an ice cube tray and place in freezing compartment of refrigerator for 10 minutes or so, stirring occasionally. Whip cream until stiff, adding a pinch of salt. Turn soup into a deep bowl, add ½ cup milk, beat with a rotary beater. Add wine and beat again. Fold in whipped cream. Serve with an ice cube or two in each bowl, and top with croutons or garnish. See end of this chapter for quick and easy garnish hints.

Serves 4 to 6

18 to 20 min.

VEGETABLE SOUP

1 cup chicken stock
1½ cups water
1 tablespoon butter
1 small onion, chopped fine
½ package frozen mixed vegetables
2 cans condensed vegetable soup, vegetarian style
salt and pepper
1 teaspoon chopped parsley

Start stock and water boiling in a saucepan over highest heat. Meanwhile melt butter in soup pot, add onion; simmer 3 minutes or until onion browns slightly. When water-stock mixture boils, add frozen mixed vegetables and cook as directed on package. When onions are ready, add canned soup and keep over low heat, stirring occasionally. When frozen vegetables are tender, add, without draining, to soup pot; combine; taste and correct seasoning with salt and pepper. Simmer 3 or 4 minutes. Sprinkle chopped parsley over each portion.

Timesaver: Instead of frozen mixed vegetables, use canned mixed vegetables, drained and rinsed in cold water. Brown onions as directed, add all ingredients; heat through, taste and correct seasoning with salt and pepper. Simmer 3 or 4 minutes and serve.

Serves 4 to 6

MAKE TWO MEALS IN ONE

Time-saver

Vegetable soup takes well to an overnight rest. So, while you're cooking *one* meal, make vegetable soup at the same time. Use the *Timesaver* method in above recipe, and just let the soup simmer on the back of the stove. Cover tightly and store in refrigerator. Next night, serve big bowls of it with hot French bread, a hearty green salad, and a chilled fruit dessert. Add a bottle of wine and you have a festive meal!

QUICK CROUTONS

10 min.

Butter both sides of 3 or 4 thin slices white bread. Rub a skillet very lightly with garlic, place bread in skillet and brown on both sides over medium heat. Dice, or cut into triangles, and serve at once. For a different touch make this with light rye bread.

SOUP GARNISH

Hints

Heat or not, as desired, 1 cup coarsely crumbled (or whole) cocktail corn chips; sprinkle over soup just before serving.

Freshen popcorn in the oven and sprinkle over soup at the table.

Most dry breakfast cereals, heated in the oven and sprinkled very lightly with salt, make attractive soup garnishes (best variety to use is crisp rice cereal).

Just before serving soup sprinkle with lightly salted cocktail shoestring potatoes, warmed in the oven.

Melt a generous tablespoon of butter in a pie tin. Add a handful of oyster crackers, toss with a spoon to coat with butter, and brown for a moment under the broiler.

Fish

Quick-Frozen Fish

Most groceries carry a good selection of frozen fish, including cod, flounder, haddock, or red perch, and sometimes salmon steaks or mackerel. Frozen shrimp, cooked or raw, are also often available. The exact variety of fish specified in a recipe need not be used. For example, cod, flounder, and haddock all have firm, white flesh, and may be interchanged. (Adjust cooking times; thicker filets need more.)

POACHED FISH FILETS WITH RIPE OLIVES

18 min.

1 cup Vichysoisse soup
1 pound flounder filets or 1 package frozen filets, thawed
milk, if needed
½ cup ripe olives, pitted
4 teaspoons flour
½ teaspoon onion juice
parsley

Measure soup into saucepan, reserving two tablespoonfuls; place over medium heat to pre-heat. Meanwhile cut fish filets into serving pieces; arrange in a large skillet; pour pre-heated soup over fish. It should barely cover; if not, add milk. Add ½ cup (or more) coarsely chopped ripe olives. Cover skillet and cook 10 minutes over medium-low heat, or until fish flakes; shake skillet occasionally to "stir." Meanwhile combine reserved soup, flour and onion juice in a small bowl; mix to a smooth paste. When fish is done, lift out onto a serving platter. Pour about ½ cup of sauce in skillet into flour-soup mixture. Stir smooth and return to sauce in skillet; stir sauce smooth. Pour over fish, sprinkle with parsley, and serve.

Serves 4 to 6

20 min.

TOMATO POACHED HADDOCK

2 8-oz. cans tomato sauce
2 teaspoons onion juice
½ cup plain chicken broth
1 teaspoon soy sauce
½ teaspoon salt; pepper
1 pound fresh haddock filets or 1 package frozen filets, thawed
¼ cup bread crumbs and ¼ cup grated cheese, mixed
butter

Start oven pre-heating to hot. Combine tomato sauce, onion juice, broth, and soy sauce in a saucepan; add salt and pepper; place over high heat until boiling, stirring occasionally. Meanwhile cut fish into 1 inch squares and place in a heatproof serving dish. Taste sauce and correct seasoning, pour over fish, and poach in oven for 10 minutes or until fish flakes when tested with a fork. Sprinkle top with crumb-cheese mixture; dot liberally with butter and brown for 2 or 3 minutes under broiler flame. Serve with rice, if desired.

Serves 4 to 6

EASY BREAD CRUMBS

Time-saver

Keep a supply of buttered bread crumbs for toppings in the refrigerator; they'll always be ready for use. Melt 2 tablespoons butter in a skillet over a low flame. Add 1½ to 2 cups bread crumbs and stir with a fork until nicely browned. Store in a covered jar. Keeps for about 2 weeks.

Note: Bread crumbs mixed with grated cheese, part for part, are also a handy topping to keep on hand. Mix up a batch and keep in your refrigerator. Keeps for several weeks stored in a covered jar.

FISH FILETS, ITALIAN STYLE

15 min.

1 10-oz. can meatless style Italian spaghetti sauce
1 8-oz. can tomato sauce
¼ cup dry white wine
garlic clove, split
pinch of oregano
1 pound flounder or haddock filets or 1 package frozen filets, thawed
plain chicken broth as needed
1 teaspoon soy sauce
salt and pepper

Combine spaghetti sauce, tomato sauce and wine in a skillet; add garlic and oregano; place over medium heat. Meanwhile cut fish into serving pieces and place in sauce, which should barely cover fish. (If not, add chicken broth.) Cover skillet and cook 10 minutes or until fish flakes when tested with a fork. Lift fish out onto serving plate, add soy sauce to skillet, mix, taste, correct seasoning with salt and pepper. Discard garlic and pour sauce over fish.

Serves 4

BROILED FISH FILETS

10 to 12 min.

(Serve with a fish sauce—see Index.)

Remove broiler pan from stove; start broiler preheating to hot. Use fresh or thawed frozen filets (best of all is lemon sole if available, or flounder). Line broiler pan with aluminum foil (or, if cooking for two, use a foil-lined pie tin). Sprinkle foil with olive oil, dust with salt and pepper. Arrange filets on foil and push fish around on foil to coat with oil and seasoning. Turn filets over and place under broiler.

For thick filets, broiling pan should be 4 to 6 inches away from heat; for thin filets, 2 to 4 inches. Broil until lightly browned. Unless filets are exceptionally thick it is not necessary to turn them.

Spread sauce of your choice over fish and serve.

Note: Fish filets cook quickly; overcooked fish is tough and stringy. Watch cooking time. Test with a fork—if fish flakes it is done.

Allow 1 filet per person

Hint

COLORFUL SALAD

Pickled beets! Nothing more colorful, and nothing better with fish! You can make them in 15 minutes and keep them for weeks in your refrigerator. You need just a spoonful or two on each plate. (See Index for recipe.)

One-dish Dinner

20 min.

FISH HASH

- 4 tablespoons butter
- 1 package frozen flounder filets
- 4 small canned onions
- 2 cups canned cooked rice
- 1 #2 can peas
- ½ cup sour cream
- salt and pepper
- celery salt
- butter

Start broiler pre-heating to hot. Melt butter in a large skillet, add fish cut in walnut-size pieces and onions, quartered. Cook over medium-high heat until fish flakes when tested with a fork (5 to 8 minutes). Meanwhile freshen rice as directed on can. Drain and rinse peas in cold water. When fish is ready, add rice and peas; mix well. Spread top with sour cream, sprinkle generously with seasonings and mix again. Dot top liberally with butter and place under broiler flame until browned (5 to 8 minutes). Serve with a green salad and hot brown-and-serve cinnamon buns; chilled fruit for dessert.

Serves 4 to 6

SOUR CREAM IN FISH COOKERY

Hint

When making fish cakes or hash, sour cream adds subtle, rich goodness. And it's thriftier! (*Note:* You can't taste the cream.)

FISH CAKES

18 min.

- 2 cups canned cooked rice
- 2 cups water
- 1 8-oz. can or more cooked canned fish(tuna, salmon, or cod)
- 2 eggs
- 1 teaspoon onion juice
- 1 tablespoon cream
- ½ teaspoon salt; pepper
- celery salt
- bread crumbs as needed

Turn rice into water and bring to a quick boil; drain. Drain liquid from fish, pick over and remove bones; flake lightly with a fork. Beat eggs lightly. Combine all ingredients but fish with rice. Be generous with seasonings. If mix is very moist, stir in up to ½ cup bread crumbs. Add fish, toss mixture lightly to combine. Drop from a spoon, or form into cakes; fry in a hot skillet, containing a generous lump of butter, until browned on both sides.

Serves 6 to 8

READY-BOILING WATER

Time-saver

Does the dish you're making use boiling water along the way? Cut a big corner this way: Before you start any cooking, put a kettle of water on over high heat. By the time you're ready, the water should be boiling; pour hot water into sauce pan when recipe says "boil" and you're minutes ahead!

15 min.

CODFISH CAKES I

- 1 egg
- 1 tablespoon cream
- 3 or 4 small canned boiled potatoes
- 1 10-oz. can prepared codfish cakes
- ½ teaspoon onion juice
- salt and pepper
- celery salt
- bread crumbs as needed

Beat egg lightly with cream. Crush potatoes in mixing bowl, add all ingredients and mix until well blended. Taste and correct seasoning. If mix is very moist, stir in a little bread crumbs. Form into cakes, and using a hot skillet, fry in butter 5 minutes to a side, or until brown.

Serves 4

20 min.

CODFISH CAKES II

- 1 5-oz. package dried, shredded codfish
- 1 #2 can boiled potatoes, drained
- 2 eggs
- 2 tablespoons cream
- 1 teaspoon onion juice
- pepper
- celery salt
- bread crumbs as needed

Refresh codfish as directed on package. Meanwhile crush potatoes with a fork and beat eggs lightly with cream. Combine all ingredients, season lightly. If mixture is very moist stir in up to ½ cup bread crumbs. Form into cakes or drop from a spoon. Fry in butter in a hot skillet, 5 minutes to a side, or until brown.

Serves 6 to 8

18 min.

CREAMED CODFISH AND MUSHROOMS

- 1 5-oz. package dried, shredded codfish
- 1 egg
- 1 teaspoon onion juice
- ¼ cup milk
- 1 can condensed cream of mushroom soup
- 1 3-oz. can mushrooms
- ¼ teaspoon salt; pepper
- paprika

Refresh codfish as directed on package. Meanwhile lightly beat together egg, onion juice, and milk; add to soup with mushrooms and mushroom liquid, salt, and a dash of pepper. Combine and heat over low heat. When fish is ready, add to mushroom mixture. Simmer 5 minutes or until thoroughly heated. Before serving (over toast if desired) taste and correct seasoning and sprinkle with paprika.

Serves 4 to 6

CODFISH CAKES AND BEANS

One-dish Dinner

1 recipe Codfish Cakes I (see above)
grated cheese
butter
½ cup chili sauce
1 #2 can baked beans, or more

Start broiler pre-heating to medium. Prepare codfish cake mixture as directed, making it firm enough to roll into walnut-size balls. Dip tops in grated cheese and arrange in a single layer on a large heatproof platter, lightly greased. Dot tops of balls liberally with butter and place under broiler 5 to 8 minutes, or until nicely browned. Meanwhile combine chili sauce and baked beans; heat thoroughly.

20 min.

To serve: pour beans all around and in between the fish balls. Serve with a hot canned brown bread, a green salad, and a whipped cream dessert.

Serves 4 to 6

FISH BOAT

One-dish Dinner

1 loaf brown-and-serve French bread
1 #2 can gefilte fish or "filled fish" balls
1 cup cooked diced carrots
1 recipe Canned Boiled Potatoes (see Index)

Brown bread in a medium oven as directed on package. Drain broth from can of fish into a saucepan; add carrots, drained and rinsed, and ¼ cup water. Place over low heat. Add fish, cut into walnut-size pieces if balls are large. Heat slowly at no more than a simmer. When bread has browned, slice off bottom crust; make diagonal cuts across the loaf from bottom to top, almost all the way through. Pull out insides (reserve for crumbs) to make a "boat." Return bread to oven for a minute or two. To serve: roll potatoes in butter and sprinkle with a little parsley. Place bread on platter and surround it with potatoes, using them as wedges to keep bread from tipping over, if needed. Heap fish and carrots into the "boat" and pour broth over. Dust very lightly with pepper. Be sure each person is served some bread and broth. Serve with a green salad and whipped cream dessert.

18 min.

Note: Ready-baked French bread may be used; heat through and remove insides as directed.

Serves 4 to 6

KNOW YOUR TUNA FISH

Hint

Always be sure to buy a well-known brand of "white meat" tuna if you want the best quality. Avoid bargains, unless you know the name on the label. You usually end up with just what you pay for.

15 min.

TUNA CREAM

4 teaspoons flour
1 cup Vichysoisse soup
¼ teaspoon salt
½ teaspoon onion juice
1 8-oz. can tuna fish
1 canned pimiento or less
1 3-oz. can mushrooms
pepper
toast slices

Measure flour into a saucepan, add 2 tablespoons soup, stir with a fork until smooth. Add salt and onion juice to remainder of soup; mix. Place flour mixture over medium heat and slowly stir in soup mixture. Cook, stirring occasionally, until sauce bubbles (about 5 minutes). Meanwhile drain tuna and break into chunks with a fork. Chop pimiento coarsely. Add well drained tuna, mushrooms, mushroom liquid, and coarsely chopped pimiento to sauce; combine; taste and correct seasoning. Heat through and serve on well-buttered brown toast.

Serves 4 to 6

TUNA CREAM IN SHELLS

15 to 18 min.

Prepare Tuna Cream (see above). First place 1 package brown-and-serve club or dinner rolls in oven to brown. When ready, slice bottoms off rolls and pull out insides to leave shells. Return to oven for 2 or 3 minutes. To serve: fill shells with hot Tuna Cream mixture, garnish with a strip of pimiento or a little parsley.

If desired, sprinkle tops of filled shells with a little grated cheese mixed with bread crumbs. Dot with butter and place under broiler heat for two or three minutes or until browned.

Serves 4 or 6

FISH SALADS

Hint

Follow Shrimp Salad recipe (see Index) for ingredients and method, substituting any canned, cooked or leftover fish for shrimp.

18 min.

TUNA RICE

2 cups canned cooked rice
1 can condensed cream of celery soup
1 teaspoon onion juice
½ cup canned bean sprouts
1 8-oz. can tuna fish, drained
salt and pepper
¼ cup bread crumbs mixed with ¼ cup grated cheese
butter

Start broiler pre-heating to medium. Freshen rice as directed on can. Meanwhile turn soup into a saucepan, stir in onion juice and bean sprouts; cook and stir occasionally over low heat. When soup is hot, add tuna fish and rice; mix; taste and correct seasoning with salt and pepper. Turn mixture into a heatproof serving dish, sprinkle with bread crumb-cheese mixture; dot generously with butter and place under broiler heat for 2 or 3 minutes or until browned.

Serves 6 to 8

18 min.

TUNA SCRAMBLE

butter
1 #2 can boiled potatoes
½ teaspoon onion juice
salt and pepper
1 8-oz. can tuna fish
6 eggs
2 tablespoons heavy cream
1 teaspoon chopped parsley

Start 2 tablespoons butter melting in a large skillet. Drain potatoes, cut in halves or quarters. Add onion juice to butter; whisk to combine; add potatoes. Dust lightly with salt and pepper. Cook and shake skillet occasionally over medium high heat for 5 minutes, or until potatoes begin to brown. Meanwhile drain tuna fish, break into large chunks. When potatoes are ready, add fish, toss to mix and turn heat to low. Beat eggs, cream, ½ teaspoon salt, a good dash of pepper, and the parsley together. Scramble in another skillet in plenty of butter. When eggs are barely set, add tuna potato mixture and scramble all together until eggs are done. Serve at once. Garnish each portion with spoonfuls of chili sauce or sour cream, if desired.

Serves 4 to 6

SALMON TOMATO BROIL

- 2 slices bread
- 1 8-oz. can salmon
- 1 small onion
- butter
- 3 tablespoons sour cream
- salt and pepper
- 4 fresh tomatoes, scooped out
- ¼ cup bread crumbs mixed with 1 tablespoon grated cheese

Start broiler pre-heating to medium. Start toast (make it brown). Drain salmon; turn into a bowl and break fish into chunks. Discard bones and skin. When toast is done, rub both sides of slices with cut surface of onion; butter lightly, cube, and add to salmon with sour cream; season rather highly with salt and pepper. Toss mixture to mix; fill tomatoes. Sprinkle tops with bread crumb-cheese mixture, dot with a little butter. Place under broiler for 10 minutes or until nicely browned.

20 min.

Timesaver: Use four or five slices melba toast instead of toasted bread. Omit onion. Add ½ teaspoon onion juice to mixture when adding sour cream.

Serves 4

HOT SALMON DISHES—VARIATIONS

SALMON RICE: Use canned salmon instead of tuna fish in recipe for Tuna Rice (see above).

SALMON SCRAMBLE: See Tuna Scramble (above). Use canned salmon instead of tuna fish.

SALMON CREAM: Substitute 1 8-oz. can, or more, salmon for tuna fish in Tuna Cream (see Index).

Note: Drain salmon well in all recipes. Remove and discard bones and skin. Since salmon is much more fragile than tuna, stir or otherwise handle the food carefully to avoid disintegration.

15 min.

SALMON SALAD

- 1 8-oz. can, or more, salmon, chilled (see Timesaver Index)
- 2 slices well-browned toast, buttered
- 2 teaspoons onion juice
- 3 tablespoons mayonnaise
- 3 tablespoons sour cream
- ¼ teaspoon salt; pepper
- celery salt

Drain liquid from salmon into a small bowl and reserve. Start toast. Turn fish into salad bowl; break into chunks, discarding skin and bones. Place bowl in refrigerator to keep cold. Combine reserved salmon liquid, onion juice, mayonnaise, sour cream, salt, and a light sprinkling of pepper and celery salt. Taste dressing and correct seasoning with salt. To serve: reserve ½ slice of toast; cut remainder into small cubes and add to salmon. Pour dressing over and toss lightly to combine. For "color" sprinkle top of salad with crumbs from reserved toast, or use garnish suggestions in Salad Ingredients (see Index).

Serves 4 to 6

18 min.

SALMON-EGG SALAD—VARIATION

Use 3 or 4 chilled hard-boiled eggs (see Timesaver Index). Mash one yolk and add to dressing for Salmon Salad (see above). Chop egg white and one additional egg; toss with salad. Garnish with egg slices.

READY-CHILLED FISH

Time-saver

Keep cans of salmon, tuna fish, crab, lobster, etc., on the back of a refrigerator shelf instead of in your cupboard. They'll be ready-chilled, any time you want them.

CHILLED SARDINES

5 min.

Have oil-pack sardines well chilled (keep a supply in your refrigerator during summer months). Open can, lift out fishes and spread out in a flat dish. Return to refrigerator. To oil in can add 1 teaspoon onion juice and a pinch of curry powder. Whisk with a fork to combine, pour over sardines. Serve on crisp lettuce leaves.

One 4-oz. can serves 1 or 2

KIPPERED HERRINGS

18 min.

- 1 15-oz. can kippered herring
- ¼ cup cream
- 1 tablespoon melted butter
- 1 teaspoon onion juice
- 1 teaspoon lemon juice
- ¼ teaspoon salt

Start broiler pre-heating to medium hot. Drain liquid from herring; trim off fins and tails; open fish flat. Combine other ingredients. Spread cream mixture on every other fish-half. Cover with another fish-half (skin side up) to make "sandwiches." Place under broiler for 6 to 10 minutes, or until well heated.

Note: Add 1 teaspoon Worcestershire sauce to cream mixture, if desired.

Serves 4

15 min.

KIPPERS IN MILK

1 15-oz. can kippered herring
milk
few slices of onion or ½ teaspoon onion juice
salt and pepper
2 teaspoons butter
boiled potatoes for the accompaniment

Drain fish, remove fins and tails. Arrange filet-halves in a large skillet and barely cover with milk. Add onion slices or onion juice, dust lightly with salt and pepper and add butter. Place over medium-low heat, cover skillet and cook 10 minutes. Serve filets without sauce, or pour sauce over hot 10-minute boiled potatoes (see Index).

Serves 4

15 min.

CREAMED SMOKED FISH

4 teaspoons flour
1 cup Vichysoisse soup
¼ teaspoon salt
½ teaspoon onion juice
parsley
½ pound smoked whitefish, carp, or other white-fleshed fish

Measure flour into a saucepan, add 2 tablespoons soup, stir with a fork until smooth. Add salt, onion juice and parsley to remainder of soup; mix. Place flour mixture over medium heat and slowly stir in soup mixture. Cook, stirring occasionally, until sauce bubbles (about 5 minutes). Meanwhile skin fish, lift flesh in large chunks from bones. Add to sauce when ready, combine gently and simmer 2 or 3 minutes. Serve over canned cooked rice, freshened as directed on can.

Note: If desired, thin sauce slightly by adding up to ⅓ cup milk when adding remainder of soup.

Serves 4

CREAMED SMOKED FISH WITH MUSHROOMS—VARIATION

Prepare above recipe as directed, adding one 3-oz. can mushroom caps, drained, to sauce when adding soup.

TO COOK RAW ("GREEN") SHRIMP

10 min.

While canned or frozen shrimp are ideal for 20-Minute Cookery, it is much more economical to cook your own if you have the extra time for shelling and deveining. Here is an easy way to do it.

1 pound shrimp (raw)
4 cups water
1 tablespoon mixed pickling spice
1 teaspoon salt
3 tablespoons wine vinegar
1 small bay leaf

Rinse shrimp in cold water. Bring all ingredients to a boil; add shrimp, and counting from when the water returns to a boil, allow 3 minutes for small shrimp, up to 5 for jumbo shrimp. Remove from heat, drain; shell and devein shrimp.

Note: For an unusually savory flavor, try adding a slashed clove of garlic to the water.

Serves 4 to 6

SHRIMP, ITALIAN STYLE

One-dish Dinner

20 min.

¼ cup dry white wine
¼ cup plain chicken broth
1 small garlic clove, split
1 3-oz. can mushrooms
1 teaspoon soy sauce
pinch of oregano
1 10-oz. can prepared spaghetti sauce, without meat
2 cups canned or frozen cooked, cleaned shrimp
salt and pepper

Combine all ingredients except prepared sauce and shrimp; bring to a fast boil. Add sauce, combine, turn heat to low; simmer 10 minutes. Add shrimp, simmer 5 minutes more. Discard garlic; taste and correct seasoning with salt and pepper. Serve over spaghetti or macaroni. Or use canned cooked rice, refreshed as directed on can.

Serves 4

One-dish Dinner

20 min.

SHRIMP BAKE

- 1 cup canned cooked rice
- ½ cup plain chicken broth
- 2 fresh tomatoes
- 2 cups canned cooked shrimp, or more
- 1 #2 can rice dinner or Spanish rice
- salt and pepper
- 4 brown-and-serve club rolls
- garlic
- butter

Start broiler pre-heating to hot. Freshen rice as directed on can. Measure chicken broth into a saucepan, add tomatoes cut in coarse chunks; place over high heat. When broth boils, turn heat to low; add cleaned, drained shrimp. Meanwhile prepare Quick Creole Sauce (see Index), using rice dinner. To serve: combine rice (which should be hot), shrimp mixture and heated sauce in a deep ovenproof serving dish. Taste and correct seasoning with salt and pepper. Cut rolls into inch-thick slices; butter lightly; rub with the faintest trace of garlic, using a cut clove. Stick bread chunks part way down into the mixture; place under broiler for 2 or 3 minutes until bread toasts.

Serves 4 to 6

15 min.

FRENCH FRIED SHRIMP

- cooking fat
- 2 cups canned or frozen cooked shrimp
- ½ cup milk
- ¾ cup biscuit mix
- salt and pepper
- celery salt
- lemon juice

Start fat pre-heating to 375°. Shell and devein shrimp. Add milk to biscuit mix; combine into a thick batter. Sprinkle shrimp with seasonings, dip each into lemon juice, then into batter. If shrimp are small, dip two together. Fry in deep fat for 3 or 4 minutes or until brown. Drain on absorbent paper and keep hot until ready to serve.

Serves 4

TO CHILL SHRIMP QUICKLY

Time-saver

Place shrimp in an ice cube tray and place in ice cube compartment of your refrigerator for 15 minutes or more, until well chilled. Do not allow to freeze.

(*Note:* Salad vegetables may be treated in the same manner. Spread thinly for quickest results.)

SHRIMP SALAD I

18 min.

garlic clove
1/3 cup French Dressing (see Index)
1/4 teaspoon onion juice, optional
1 cup chilled canned mixed vegetables
2 cups canned or frozen cooked shrimp, cleaned and chilled
Salad Greens (see Index)

Rub salad bowl lightly with garlic. Add dressing (use a little more than 1/3 cup, if desired), onion juice, vegetables, well-drained shrimp; combine by tossing. Drain off and reserve excess dressing; put shrimp mixture in refrigerator. Toss greens with reserved dressing. To serve: arrange a bed of greens in salad bowl; place shrimp mixture in center (discard garlic); garnish with chilled hard-cooked egg quarters or slices, or tomato wedges, or tomatoes and eggs both. Sprinkle garnish very lightly with salt and pepper and spoon a little dressing over. Or, if garnish is not at hand, chop greens coarsely before adding dressing; toss together with shrimp mixture.

Note: If shrimp (or vegetables) are not chilled, see above for a quick way. Combine with dressing first; then chill.

Serves 4

One-dish Dinner

SHRIMP SALAD II

2 tablespoons mayonnaise
⅓ cup sour cream
split garlic clove
pinch nutmeg
½ teaspoon celery seed
½ teaspoon salt; pepper
2 cups canned shrimp, chilled
Salad Greens (see Index)

15 min.

Combine first 6 ingredients in a salad bowl rubbed with garlic. Add shrimp, combine; add chopped salad greens; toss together and serve—with a bottle of cooled dry white wine, hot French bread, and a whipped cream dessert.

Serves 4

Hint

CRAB OR LOBSTER MEAT

For salads or hot dishes, use canned or frozen-cooked lobster or crab meat. Many markets carry fresh cooked crab or lobster, removed from the shell and ready to eat.

Use crab or lobster meat with or in place of shrimp.

Fowl

BROILED FROZEN CHICKEN BREASTS

1 package (4) frozen chicken breasts
2 cups water
1 tablespoon lemon juice
olive oil
salt and pepper

Chicken should be thawed enough for pieces to separate. Start broiler pre-heating to very hot. Measure water and lemon juice into a saucepan and place over highest heat to boil. Separate pieces, pull off skin, rinse under running cold water and drop into boiling water. Keep over high heat; cook 3 minutes by the clock. Meanwhile, coat a foil-lined pie tin generously with olive oil; sprinkle well with salt and pepper. When chicken breasts have cooked for 3 minutes, drain and discard water. Push pieces of chicken around on foil to coat both sides with oil and seasonings. Broil 6 to 8 minutes to a side, or until nicely browned. Salt lightly before serving with a pat of butter melting on each portion.

20 min.

Serves 3 or 4

THAWED-IN-ADVANCE FROZEN FOODS

Time-saver

How about asking your grocer to help? Take frozen chicken breasts, for example. If you haven't shopped ahead of time, why not call your grocer early in the day that you're going to use the food, and ask him to remove the package from his freezer. By the time you pick up the food later in the day, it will be thawed enough to give you a big headstart. (This idea works fine with frozen fish, too!)

CHICKEN ON THE GARLIC SIDE

If you're a skeptic when it comes to garlic, next time you broil chicken (or meat or fish) try this on one corner of one piece, just for a taste test.

Hints

Cut a clove of garlic across, into halves. Just whisk —but *only* whisk—the cut surface of the garlic over the chicken after it is cooked and ready to serve. Now add a bit of butter and let it melt. Taste—and see if you don't go back and season all the rest of the food this way!

CANNED COOKED FOWL

Canned half- or whole-pack chicken is usually liberally supplied with gravy. If there is too much for your taste, reserve some for another dish; it makes an excellent sauce base. Keep extra gravy well refrigerated.

Hints

When seasoning any canned chicken, boned or pieces, keep in mind that the chicken is *already* richly flavored. Don't overseason; be especially wary of salt. Taste as you go.

A touch of onion helps to cut back an over-rich chicken flavor. When heating, add a little onion juice or a fresh onion cut in halves or quarters. Discard onion pieces before serving.

The meat of canned cooked fowl is very tender, and will break into bits while being cooked, unless handled carefully. If the dish you're making is to be stirred, use a large spoon, and fold, rather than stir.

SEASONING SUGGESTIONS FOR READY-TO-SERVE FOWL DISHES

(CHICKEN & NOODLES, CHICKEN FRICASSEE, CREAMED CHICKEN, ETC.)

Add 1 teaspoon dried celery flakes.

Add ½ teaspoon dried chopped parsley.

Add no more than ⅛ teaspoon curry powder.

Add extra chicken, leftover or cooked and boned.

While chicken is heating, sauté until soft a few thin slices of onion in a little butter; add a 3-oz. can of mushroom caps, drained. Combine and add to chicken.

Rub a square inch of the pan lightly with garlic before starting to heat chicken.

Hints

TO EXTEND CANNED READY-TO-SERVE FOWL DISHES

Add up to ¾ cup canned Chinese bean sprouts, well drained.

Add up to ¾ cup cooked peas, or peas and carrots.

Note: When extending canned ready-to-serve fowl dishes, thin sauce slightly. To avoid disintegration of the tender chicken pieces: spoon as much sauce from the can as possible; heat and thin in a separate pan, adding extender. Meanwhile heat chicken in another pan. Combine sauce and chicken and simmer a moment or two before serving.

Hints

TURKEY OR OTHER CANNED COOKED FOWL

Hint

Substitute any variety of canned, cooked fowl quantity for quantity in any recipe. When cooking for a large group, check the price on canned turkey as compared with canned chicken. Sometimes it pays to buy a large-size can of solid turkey meat rather than several cans of chicken.

12 min.

CREAMED CHICKEN

4 teaspoons flour
1 cup Vichysoisse soup
¼ teaspoon salt
½ teaspoon onion juice
1 6-oz. can boned chicken

Measure flour into saucepan; add 2 tablespoons soup, salt, and onion juice; stir until smooth. Place over medium heat and slowly stir in remainder of soup. Cook, stirring occasionally, until sauce bubbles (about 5 minutes). Add chicken with its broth, and break into chunks. Combine gently. Heat through and serve.

Note: If desired, add one 3-oz. can mushroom caps, drained, when adding chicken to sauce; or 1 pimiento, chopped; or, just before serving, stir in half a small green pepper cut into thumbnail size bits and cooked in a little butter until soft.

Serves 4 to 6

PLAN YOUR LEFTOVERS

Time-saver

For example, creamed chicken keeps well. So make some extra (even *double* the recipe). Next night, serve mashed potatoes for dinner, and also make some extra. The third night you're all set to whip up Chicken Patties (see Index) in minutes!

Note: Leftovers stored in any refrigerator should be

well wrapped with waxed paper. Always taste leftover food before using; make certain it is still fresh.

HOW TO MAKE TOAST THAT'S *REALLY* CRISP

(*For Creamed or Gravied Fowl Dishes*)

Hint

Before putting bread in toaster, cut through crust at half-inch intervals all around. Then toast to a light brown. (If you don't have an automatic toaster it takes about 2 minutes to toast one side of a bread slice.) Allow toast to cool, unbuttered. Just before you're ready to use it, pop toast in toaster again for a half-minute or so, to heat it. It will be nicely crisp.

Timesaver: Use warmed Melba toast, broken into small squares.

CHICKEN DE LUXE

20 min.

- 1 package (6) brown-and-serve club or other large-size rolls
- 1 recipe Creamed Chicken (see above)
- 1 3-oz. can mushroom bits and pieces
- 12 to 16 green pimiento-stuffed olives
- bread crumbs mixed with grated cheese

Start oven pre-heating to 375° and brown rolls as directed on package. Meanwhile prepare Creamed Chicken, add mushrooms, drained, and olives, coarsely chopped. When rolls are brown, cut thin slices off bottoms and pull out insides of rolls to make shells. Return shells to oven for two minutes. Pile chicken mixture into shells, sprinkle tops with bread crumb-cheese mixture. Brown lightly under a hot broiler.

Serves 4 to 6

20 min.

CHICKEN, RISSOTO STYLE

1 6-oz. box packaged pre-cooked rice
1 #2 can whole-pack tomatoes
chicken broth
1 6-oz. can boned chicken
1 3-oz. can mushrooms
pinch of saffron
salt and pepper
butter

See rice package for amount of water required to cook rice; make up liquid by draining juice from tomatoes into measuring cup and adding chicken broth. Pour liquid into a large saucepan, add rice, and bring to a boil over high heat. Meanwhile break chicken into coarse chunks; cut tomatoes into eighths. When rice mixture is boiling add chicken, tomatoes, mushrooms and saffron. Taste broth and correct seasoning with salt and pepper. Cook as directed for rice (see package). Just before serving, stir in a generous chunk of butter.

Serves 4

18 min.

CHICKEN CURRY RICE

1 6-oz. box packaged pre-cooked rice
½ cup chicken broth
water
1 teaspoon curry powder
1 canned cooked half-chicken
salt and pepper

Cook rice as directed on package, using chicken broth as part of liquid, and adding curry powder. Meanwhile cut chicken into serving pieces and heat thoroughly in can gravy. Add a pinch or two of curry powder to gravy, if desired. To serve: make a rice ring (see Timesaver Index) and fill center with chicken; spoon over about ½ cup gravy, reserving remainder for another dish. Or, make a layer of rice on the bottom of a warmed shallow serving dish, reserving 1 cup. Arrange chicken on top, sprinkle with reserved rice, spoon a little gravy over and garnish with chopped parsley.

Serves 3 or 4

CHICKEN, CHILI STYLE

18 min.

- 1 cup chicken broth
- ½ cup packaged precooked rice
- 1 fresh tomato, chopped
- 3 tablespoons tomato sauce
- 6 canned baby onions, crushed
- 1 5-oz. can boned chicken
- butter
- 1 or 2 teaspoons chili powder
- salt and pepper

Measure broth into saucepan and place over high heat. When it boils, add all ingredients except chicken, butter, and seasonings. Simmer 10 minutes with a cover on the pot. Add chicken, break into chunks with a fork, add a pat of butter and chili powder; combine; taste and correct seasoning with salt and pepper. Simmer 2 or 3 minutes and serve.

Note: If desired, omit rice; serve on the side, making enough for 4. Sauce will then be thin; thicken slightly with 1 teaspoon flour creamed with 1 teaspoon butter.

Serves 4

CHICKEN PATTIES

15 min.

- 1 cup leftover Creamed Chicken (see Index)
- 1 cup mashed potatoes
- 1 egg, lightly beaten
- bread crumbs
- salt and pepper
- butter

Combine creamed chicken and mashed potatoes. Stir in egg and add enough bread crumbs to make a stiff mixture. Shape into patties, after tasting and correcting seasoning with salt and pepper. Fry in a hot skillet in plenty of butter, about 5 minutes to a side or until nicely browned. Serve with Quick Rich Cream Sauce or Mushroom Sauce (see Index).

Makes 6 to 8

18 min.

CHICKEN HASH

- butter
- 1 #2 can boiled baby potatoes
- 1 6-oz. can boned chicken
- 1 teaspoon onion juice
- ½ teaspoon each, pepper, celery salt, chopped parsley
- 4 tablespoons sour cream

Start broiler pre-heating to hot. Melt a generous chunk of butter in a heavy skillet; add potatoes which have been drained, rinsed, and halved. Add chicken broken into coarse pieces; cook over medium heat 5 minutes, stirring occasionally. Meanwhile stir onion juice and seasonings into sour cream; spread over hash when ready; mix. Cook two or three minutes more; dot top generously with butter and brown under broiler for 3 to 5 minutes.

Serves 4 to 6

One-dish Dinner

20 min.

CHICKEN PIE WITH BISCUIT TOPPING

- 1 cup chicken broth
- ½ package frozen peas and carrots
- 1 recipe Biscuits (see Index)
- 1 12-oz. can creamed chicken
- 1 can boiled baby potatoes
- 1 6-oz. can boned chicken
- salt and pepper
- onion juice

Start oven pre-heating to temperature noted on biscuit mix package. Measure broth into saucepan and place over high heat; when boiling add frozen vegetables; cook as directed on vegetable package. Meanwhile prepare and bake biscuits. When vegetable is cooked, do not drain. Add creamed chicken, stir smooth, then add potatoes drained and rinsed in cold water, and boned chicken broken into chunks. Combine, taste and correct seasoning with salt and pepper; add a few drops of onion juice if needed. Keep over low heat until biscuits are baked. To serve: turn into a casserole, top with biscuits and let a bit of butter melt on each biscuit.

Timesaver: Use canned ready-to-bake biscuits instead of biscuit-mix recipe.

Note: When extra time is available, chicken mixture may be turned into a casserole, topped with unbaked biscuits, and baked as the classic chicken pie.

Serves 4 to 6

CHICKEN PIE WITH BISCUIT TOPPING—VARIATIONS

20 min.

CHICKEN PIE, SHORTCAKE STYLE: Prepare Chicken Pie with Biscuit Topping (see above) but serve this way: when biscuits are baked, split them and make a layer of biscuit bottoms edge to edge on a serving dish. Heap on chicken mixture, reserving a little. Add tops of biscuits. Spoon reserved chicken into crevices between biscuits. Garnish with fresh parsley or sprinkle lightly with chopped dehydrated parsley, or dust lightly with paprika.

20 min.

CREAMED CHICKEN RING: Prepare Chicken Pie with Biscuit Topping (see above). Turn a pie or cake tin upside down, or use a cookie sheet; arrange raw biscuits in a circle with edges touching, leaving a 5 inch opening in center of ring. When baked, loosen ring with a spatula and slide in one piece onto serving dish. Fill center with creamed chicken mixture. Especially attractive when biscuits are made "drop" style (see Timesaver Index).

18 min.

CHICKEN PAPRIKA I

- 1 recipe Creamed Chicken (see Index)
- 1 or 2 fresh tomatoes, chopped
- ¼ cup tomato sauce
- 8 or 10 pitted black olives, chopped
- 1 to 2 teaspoons sweet paprika
- ⅓ cup sour cream

When sauce in creamed chicken bubbles, add tomatoes, tomato sauce, olives and paprika. Combine; simmer 5 minutes. Add chicken as directed in basic recipe and simmer 5 minutes more. Stir in sour cream at the last minute before serving—over rice, if desired.

Serves 4 to 6

20 min.

CHICKEN PAPRIKA II—WHOLE STYLE

For half chicken

- 1 canned cooked half chicken
- ½ teaspoon onion juice
- 1 or 2 fresh tomatoes
- ½ cup tomato sauce
- 2 or 3 teaspoons sweet paprika
- sour cream

For whole chicken

- 1 canned cooked whole chicken
- 1 teaspoon onion juice
- 2 or 3 fresh tomatoes
- 1 cup tomato sauce
- 3 or 4 teaspoons sweet paprika
- sour cream

Start broiler pre-heating to medium. Pour liquid from chicken into a large saucepan and place over medium heat. Cut chicken into serving pieces, discarding skin; arrange on broiler pan and place under broiler to heat and brown for about 10 minutes. Add onion juice, tomatoes, tomato sauce and paprika to gravy from chicken. When chicken is ready, return it to gravy, simmer 2 or 3 minutes, remove from heat and stir in about ½ cup sour cream. Serve immediately, over rice if desired. Chopped black olives make an excellent garnish.

Note: If less sauce is desired, remove ½ cup chicken liquid before adding seasonings. Reserve liquid for another dish.

Half chicken serves 3 or 4

Whole chicken serves 4 to 6

CHICKEN STEW

One-dish Dinner

- ½ cup chicken broth
- 1 cup water
- 1 canned cooked half chicken
- 1 package frozen mixed vegetables
- 1 #2 can boiled baby potatoes
- 8 or 10 canned baby onions
- celery salt
- salt and pepper

20 min.

Bring broth and water to a boil, over highest heat. Turn chicken and gravy into a saucepan and place over medium heat. When broth and water are boiling, add mixed vegetables and cook as directed on package. Drain and rinse potatoes and onions. When mixed vegetables are tender, add potatoes and onions; heat through. Lift chicken from its gravy, using a slotted spoon, and add to vegetable mixture with ½ cup chicken gravy or slightly more; reserve the remainder for another dish. Combine, taste and correct seasoning with celery salt, salt and pepper, and serve.

Serves 4 to 6

CHICKEN, POLENTA STYLE

20 min.

- 1½ cups water
- ¼ teaspoon salt
- ⅓ cup cornmeal
- 2 tablespoons butter
- 1 small onion
- 1 garlic clove, split
- 1 canned cooked half chicken
- 1 3-oz. can tomato sauce
- 1 3-oz. can mushroom caps
- 1 teaspoon soy sauce
- salt and pepper

Put water over highest heat, add salt; when boiling slowly stir in cornmeal; reduce heat to low, cover pot and cook 15 minutes, stirring occasionally.

Melt butter in a large saucepan, add coarsely chopped onion and garlic. Simmer 3 or 4 minutes until onion is soft. Meanwhile drain gravy from chicken and reserve for another dish; remove and discard skin and bones from chicken, keeping the meat in large chunks. When onion is ready, discard garlic, add chicken, tomato sauce, mushroom caps, soy sauce and light seasonings. Simmer slowly 10 minutes, carefully stirring occasionally. Taste and correct seasoning when ready. To serve: spoon most of the cornmeal onto a platter, place chicken pieces over and spoon on remaining cornmeal. Pour sauce over.

Serves 4

Hint

READY-PREPARED FOWL STUFFINGS

Many stores now sell prepared fowl stuffing, consisting of bread crumbs and seasonings. If you like less seasoning, or would rather have your own, soak stuffing mix in hot water for 5 minutes, squeeze dry, discard water, and start your own recipe. Since stuffing will already be moistened, add less liquid than recipe calls for.

Note: A few tablespoons of sour cream added to packaged stuffing mix (or any fowl stuffing) work wonders with the flavor and richness.

20 min.

"CHICKEN WITH THE STUFFING ON TOP"

- 1 small clove garlic, split
- 2 tablespoons butter
- 1 teaspoon onion juice
- 1 canned cooked whole or half chicken
- pepper; paprika
- 1 recipe Chicken Stuffing Tidbits (see following recipe)

Start oven pre-heating to 425°. In a small saucepan, lightly rubbed with garlic, melt butter and stir in onion juice. Remove from heat. Drain as much gravy as possible from chicken and arrange in a shallow pan, either whole or cut into serving portions. Brush with the butter mixture, dust lightly with pepper and paprika, and place in oven for 15 minutes or until slightly browned. Baste occasionally with pan juices, spooning out excessive liquid if it appears in the pan. Place ½ cup of the chicken gravy over low heat. If desired, seasoning may be adjusted with a few drops of onion juice, ¼ teaspoon dried celery flakes and a generous pinch of chopped parsley. If gravy is thin it may be thickened with 1 teaspoon flour creamed with 2 teaspoons butter. Have gravy piping hot. To serve: strew Chicken Stuffing Tidbits, which have been prepared meanwhile, over the browned chicken, or serve as a side dish, with a liberal helping for each person. Serve gravy on the side.

Note: For crisper browning, place chicken under medium broiler heat to finish, after it has been in the oven 10 to 12 minutes.

Serves 3 to 6

CHICKEN STUFFING TIDBITS

15 min.

½ cup chicken broth
¼ teaspoon thyme
¼ teaspoon ground sage
¼ teaspoon celery salt
⅛ teaspoon salt
1 egg
½ teaspoon onion juice
⅛ teaspoon pepper
4 slices thin white bread
butter

Measure half the chicken broth into a saucepan, add thyme, sage, celery salt and salt; when it simmers remove from heat. Meanwhile, beat egg with remaining broth, onion juice and pepper, using a rotary beater. Now trim crusts from bread, cut slices into 4 strips, then across 4 times to make tiny squares. Stir heated broth into egg, beat with rotary beater, turn bread into egg mixture and let soak for a minute or so. Melt a generous chunk of butter in a large skillet. Dip bread squares from egg liquid with a slotted spoon, allowing them to drain; turn into skillet. Arrange in a single layer and fry over medium heat 3 to 5 minutes to a side, or until nicely browned.

Serves 4

OTHER WAYS TO SERVE CHICKEN STUFFING TIDBITS

Hint

With Creamed Chicken (see Index). Instead of cubing bread, cut each slice across to make 4 triangles. Serve chicken in individual casseroles with triangles tucked into the sides of each portion.

With Chicken Salad I or II (see Index) tidbits are ideal as the "hot" side dish for a cold summer meal.

As a changeover topping for Chicken Pie (see Index), turn chicken mixture into casserole and serve with tidbits piled on top.

18 min.

HOT OPEN-FACE CHICKEN SANDWICH

2 tablespoons butter
1 tablespoon flour
½ cup water
½ cup chicken broth
½ teaspoon onion juice
¼ teaspoon celery salt
salt and pepper
1 6-oz. can boned chicken
1 3-oz. can mushroom caps, drained

Melt butter in a saucepan, add flour and blend smooth. Slowly add water and chicken broth, stirring constantly until smooth. Add onion juice and seasonings; combine; add chicken and mushrooms, broken into coarse chunks. Keep over very low heat, stirring occasionally. Meanwhile prepare Chicken Stuffing Tidbits (see above), cutting each slice of bread diagonally across into 2 triangles. Cook as directed. To serve: arrange two tidbit triangles on each plate; lift chicken from gravy with a slotted spoon and drain slightly; pile chicken on tidbits and spoon gravy over.

Serves 4

THRIFTY CHICKEN BROTH

Time-saver

To 2½ cups boiling water add 3 chicken bouillon cubes. When dissolved, cool, bottle, and keep in refrigerator. Use as needed when recipes call for chicken broth. Stir or shake before measuring out broth wanted. Keeps for several days.

CHICKEN SALAD I

15 to 20 min.

- 1 6-oz. can boned chicken, chilled
- ½ cup French Dressing (see Index)
- ½ cup finely chopped celery
- salt and pepper
- celery salt
- Chopped Salad Vegetables (see Index) to make 2 cups

Break chicken into chunks, turn into salad bowl; add dressing and celery. Toss lightly to coat with dressing; drain off and reserve excess dressing and place chicken in refrigerator while preparing vegetables. Just before serving, toss vegetables with reserved dressing, add to chicken mixture and toss again. Taste and correct seasoning with salt, pepper, and celery salt. Serve on a bed of crisp greens over which a little dressing has been dribbled.

Serves 4

QUICK AND PRETTY CRANBERRY GARNISH FOR CHICKEN SALAD

Hint

Use jellied cranberry sauce—the 4-oz. can makes plenty. Remove both ends of the can and turn the jelly onto a plate. Dice (see Index), and sprinkle over each portion of salad, or over top of salad bowl.

CHICKEN SALAD II

10 to 15 min.

- 1 small clove of garlic
- ¼ cup mayonnaise
- ¼ cup sour cream
- 2 tablespoons heavy sweet cream
- ½ teaspoon celery seed
- ¼ teaspoon salt; pepper
- 1 6-oz. can boned chicken, chilled
- Chopped Salad Vegetables (see Index) to make 2 cups

Combine all ingredients except chicken and vegetables in a salad bowl lightly rubbed with garlic. Add chicken, broken into chunks; toss. Place bowl in refrigerator until ready to serve. Add vegetables and toss again. Taste and correct seasoning with salt and pepper before serving.

Serves 4

CHICKEN SALAD II—VARIATION

15 to 20 min.

CHICKEN SALAD STUFFED IN TOMATOES: Carefully scoop out insides of 4 large, ripe tomatoes, which should be chilled. Chop insides coarsely and add to salad vegetables. Fill tomatoes with chicken salad, omitting 1 cup of salad vegetables from the recipe.

Meat

MINUTE STEAKS WITH MUSHROOM SAUCE

15 min.

1 3-oz. can mushrooms
¼ teaspoon soy sauce
water
1 tablespoon butter
1 tablespoon flour
½ beef bouillon cube
salt and pepper
1 or 2 packages (2 or 4) frozen minute steaks

Drain mushroom liquid into measuring cup; add soy sauce and water to make ½ cup. Melt butter in saucepan, add flour, stir smooth. Add water mixture slowly, cooking and stirring over medium heat until smooth. Add bouillon cube and mushrooms; combine; taste and correct seasoning with salt and pepper. Keep over low heat until wanted. Broil or pan fry steaks as directed on package (thin frozen meat may be cooked without thawing). When steaks are done, add pan juices to mushroom sauce, stir well, and pour over steak.

Serves 2 to 4

MINUTE STEAKS WITH ONION SAUCE

15 min.

¾ cup water
½ package dehydrated onion soup mix (see below)
2 teaspoons flour
2 teaspoons butter
¼ teaspoon sugar
1 or 2 packages (2 or 4) frozen minute steaks
pan drippings

Bring water to a boil in a saucepan, add soup mix, simmer 8 minutes. Cream flour and butter together. Add to soup mix and stir until smooth. Add sugar.

Cook steaks as directed on package. To make drippings add a pat of butter to the pan. Add drippings to sauce, mix well, and pour over steak.

Serves 2 or 4

Time-saver

TO MEASURE OUT HALF A PACKAGE OF DEHYDRATED SOUP

If the seasoning powder in the package is granular, or breaks apart easily, turn soup mix into a bowl, and stir powder through thoroughly. Put a spoonful back into the envelope, another spoonful into a cup, and repeat, until evenly divided.

If seasoning in soup is in a sausage-like roll, cut roll in half. Divide remaining mix by spoonfuls, or judge it with your eye.

To store unused soup, fold envelope edge over several times to make a tight seal and place package in refrigerator.

One-dish Dinner

20 min.

INDIVIDUAL MEAT PIES

6 large brown-and-serve rolls
½ package frozen peas
2 tablespoons butter
2 tablespoons flour
1 cup water
1 beef bouillon cube
¼ teaspoon celery salt
1 teaspoon chopped parsley
1 cup or more canned boiled baby potatoes
2 cans hamburgers, brown gravy style
salt and pepper

Start oven pre-heating to 375°. Start browning rolls. Start peas cooking, following package directions. Melt butter in a saucepan, stir in flour, add water slowly, stirring constantly to make a smooth sauce. Add beef bouillon cube, celery salt, parsley, potatoes drained and rinsed, and hamburgers cut into eighths. Combine; add cooked peas, drained; taste and correct seasoning with salt and pepper. Simmer until heated through. Cut bottoms off rolls, pull out insides to make shells; return to oven for 2 minutes. Pile mixture into shells and serve.

Timesaver: Omit butter, flour, water, bouillon cube, celery salt. Use 1 11-oz. can gravy instead. Omit frozen peas; use 1 cup or more canned peas, drained and rinsed. Combine all ingredients in recipe and heat through before serving.

Makes 6

WAXED PAPER THAT REALLY COVERS

Time-saver

Fold a sheet of waxed paper double, and pat it into place right on top of the food you're storing in the refrigerator—even soup. The paper goes on in seconds—stays put—and the food keeps much better.

HAMBURGER, ITALIAN STYLE

One-dish Dinner

1 package spaghetti dinner
1 or 2 cans hamburgers, tomato sauce style
1 3-oz. can mushrooms
1 teaspoon onion juice
1 garlic clove, split
oregano
salt and pepper
grated cheese

18 min.

Start broiler pre-heating to medium. Put on to boil quantity of water called for on spaghetti dinner package (see Index). Cook spaghetti as directed. Meanwhile, in a saucepan combine hamburgers cut in quarters, hamburger gravy, sauce from spaghetti dinner, mushrooms and mushroom liquid, onion juice, garlic, and a generous pinch of oregano. Heat through, discard garlic, taste and correct seasoning with salt and pepper. To serve: turn spaghetti into a heatproof casserole, reserving a little. Pile meat mixture on top; spread on reserved spaghetti. Sprinkle very lightly with grated cheese and brown under the broiler for a minute or two. Serve with extra grated cheese.

Serves 4 to 6

One-dish Dinner

HAMBURGER STEW

- ½ cup water
- ½ cup canned beef gravy
- 1 can condensed vegetable soup
- 1 cup canned boiled baby potatoes
- 1 cup canned peas and carrots
- ½ teaspoon chopped parsley
- 1 or 2 cans hamburgers, brown gravy style
- salt and pepper

15 min.

Add water and gravy to soup; combine and place over medium heat. Add canned vegetables, rinsed in cold water. (If potatoes are small, use whole; otherwise halved or quartered.) When mixture is hot, add parsley, hamburgers, quartered, and can gravy. Combine; taste and correct seasoning with salt and pepper; heat through and serve in bowls with hot French bread. Sprinkle each portion with more parsley, if desired.

Note: This recipe makes a thick stew. To thin, use more canned gravy or add beef broth.

Serves 4

18 min.

BARBECUED HAMBURGERS

- 1 8-oz. can tomato sauce
- 1 teaspoon onion juice
- 1 clove garlic, split
- 1 tablespoon Worcestershire sauce
- 2 tablespoons brown sugar
- 1 or 2 tablespoons wine vinegar
- 3 tablespoons chili sauce
- pinch of dry mustard
- salt and pepper
- 2 cans hamburgers, tomato sauce style

Combine all ingredients except hamburgers, including gravy from cans. Simmer 10 minutes; taste and correct seasoning with salt, pepper, and a little granulated sugar, if needed. Discard garlic. Add hamburgers, heat through, and serve.

Serves 4 to 6

HAMBURGERS WITH ONION SAUCE

20 min.

- 2 half-pound packages frozen chopped beef (4 patties)
- salt and pepper
- garlic clove
- olive oil
- onion sauce

Rub meat lightly with salt and pepper, then with cut clove of garlic. Place in a hot skillet with a little olive oil and cook over medium heat 6 to 8 minutes to a side, or until done. Meanwhile prepare onion sauce, as in Minute Steaks with Onion Sauce or Onion Sauce for Meat (see Index). To serve: turn hamburgers onto serving dish; pour sauce into skillet; scrape bottom of skillet with a spatula. Stir sauce and simmer for a half-minute or so. Pour over meat.

Serves 3 or 4

TO MAKE WELL-DONE FROZEN CHOPPED MEAT

Time-saver

Season meat as directed in recipe above; cook both sides until brown, using a hot skillet. Just before ready to serve, lift patties onto a plate; hold pattie on edge with a pair of kitchen tongs, and using a sharp knife, cut into two slices. Return to skillet, rare side down. Meat will finish cooking in 2 or 3 minutes. Serve with pan juices.

TOMATOBURGERS

18 min.

- 2 large firm tomatoes
- salt and pepper
- butter
- 2 cans hamburgers, tomato sauce style
- 1 3-oz. can mushrooms
- 1 teaspoon onion juice
- pat of butter

Start broiler pre-heating to medium. Cut tomatoes into 8 thick slices and place in a lightly greased pie tin; sprinkle with salt and pepper and top each slice with a generous bit of butter. Place under hot broiler; cook tomatoes about 10 minutes. Meanwhile pour gravy from hamburger can into a skillet, add mushrooms and mushroom liquid, onion juice and pat of butter. Place over medium heat and mix well. Slice hamburgers in half horizontally and place cut sides down in sauce. Heat through. To serve: make sandwiches using tomato slices as the "filling," hamburger halves top and bottom. Spoon sauce over.

Serves 4 to 6

20 min.

BEEF AND SNAP BEANS, SPANISH STYLE

Prepare Snap Beans Spanish style (see Index) with this variation: when beans have cooked about 10 minutes, add 1 can hamburgers, tomato sauce style. Quarter the hamburgers, if desired.

Serves 3 or 4

18 min.

HAMBURGERS, STROGANOFF STYLE

- 2 tablespoons butter
- 1 tablespoon flour
- 1 cup hot water and one whole-pack canned tomato, or ½ cup water and ¾ cup tomato sauce
- 1 teaspoon onion juice
- 1 beef bouillon cube
- 2 cans hamburgers, brown gravy style
- 1 3-oz. can mushrooms, drained
- ½ cup sour cream

Melt butter in skillet, add flour, stir smooth. Add water, onion juice, bouillon cube, gravy from meat, and mushrooms; cook and stir over medium heat until smooth. Add tomato cut into chunks, or tomato sauce; mix well. Add meat and simmer 10 minutes. Just before serving remove meat to serving dish; stir sour cream into sauce and pour over meat. Serve at once.

Serves 4 to 6

STROGANOFF TARTS

20 min.

Start oven pre-heating to medium; place six large brown-and-serve rolls in oven to brown. Prepare Hamburgers, Stroganoff style (see above); cut hamburgers into eighths, or crush into coarse chunks, using a fork. When rolls are ready, slice off bottoms and pull out insides to make shells. Return shells to oven for two minutes. Add the ½ cup sour cream to meat mixture; combine, and fill shells. Top with a bit of butter and place under high broiler heat for 2 or 3 minutes. Just before serving top each portion with a spoonful of sour cream and sprinkle with a little chopped parsley.

Makes 6

MEAT STEWS—"HOME-COOKED" BASE

20 min.

- 2 tablespoons butter
- 1 stalk celery, chopped
- 1 teaspoon onion juice
- 1 cup or more canned baby potatoes
- 1 cup canned peas and carrots
- ½ cup chicken broth
- ½ teaspoon parsley
- ¼ teaspoon salt; pepper

Melt butter in a saucepan, add celery; cook 5 minutes over medium heat. Rinse vegetables under cold water and add with all other ingredients. Heat through. Add as directed in stew recipes.

Note: If time permits, use ½ package cooked frozen peas and carrots instead of canned.

Serves 2 or 3 when added to one #2 can or 1 package frozen stew

HOW TO SPEED UP MEAT STEW PREPARATION

Time-saver

Use our two-pan method: in *one* pan, prepare the base (see above) that adds the home-cooked touch to ready-cooked stew; in a *second* pan, and at the same time, heat the prepared stew mixture. Combine the base and the stew; simmer for 2 or 3 minutes, and serve.

BEEF STEW

One-dish Dinner

Before starting "Home-Cooked" Stew Base (see above), bring ¼ cup water to a boil in a saucepan; add canned or frozen beef stew. (If frozen, cook for a minute or so; turn block over and cook another minute or two. Break into chunks, using a knife point.) Cook stew over medium heat, stirring occasionally. Now prepare stew base. When stew is heated through, add to base; combine; taste and correct seasoning; simmer 2 or 3 minutes and serve.

LAMB STEW

One-dish Dinner

Before starting "Home-Cooked" Stew Base (see above), bring ¼ cup water to a boil in a saucepan; add canned or frozen lamb stew. (If frozen, cook for a minute or so; turn block over and cook another minute or two. Break into chunks, using a knife point.) Cook stew over medium low heat, stirring occasionally. Now prepare stew base adding with the mixed vegetables 1 3-oz. can mushroom caps, drained, and a pinch of thyme or oregano. When stew has heated through, combine with base; taste and correct seasoning; simmer 2 or 3 minutes, and serve.

VEAL STEW

One-dish Dinner

Start 1 can veal stew heating, adding ¼ cup water and the tip of a bayleaf. Then prepare "Home-Cooked" Stew Base (see above). When stew has heated through, combine with base, add a generous shake of paprika and 3 tablespoons sour cream. Combine; taste and correct seasoning with salt and pepper. Keep over low heat (do not boil) for 2 or 3 minutes and serve.

VEAL, PAPRIKA STYLE

One-dish Dinner

20 min.

- ¼ cup water
- 1 package frozen or 1 can veal stew
- 2 tablespoons butter
- 1 small onion, chopped
- pinch of oregano or thyme
- 2 teaspoons sweet paprika
- ½ cup sour cream
- ¼ teaspoon salt; pepper

Bring ¼ cup water to a boil in a saucepan; add stew. (If frozen, cook for a minute or two, turn block over and cook another minute or two. Break into chunks, using a knife point.) In another saucepan melt butter, add onion and simmer 5 minutes. Add remainder of ingredients and stew; mix well; heat for 5 minutes, but do not boil. Taste, correct seasoning with salt and pepper and serve.

Serves 2 or 3

BEEF GOULASH

One-dish Dinner

- ¼ cup water
- Half a beef bouillon cube
- 1 can beef goulash
- 1 cup cooked carrots
- 4 canned boiled baby potatoes or more, diced
- ½ teaspoon sweet paprika
- 1 teaspoon onion juice
- salt and pepper
- ½ cup sour cream

15 min.

Bring water to a boil in a saucepan; add bouillon cube and goulash. When stew is heated, add all ingredients except sour cream and mix well. Cook and stir occasionally over medium heat for 5 minutes or until well heated. Just before serving, taste and correct seasoning with salt and pepper; stir in sour cream. If desired, serve each portion topped with a spoonful of sour cream.

Serves 4

GET ALL THE GRAVY

Hint

Often some of the gravy packed with canned meats remains congealed in the bottom of the can. Be sure to look for it—and to get all the goodness, add 1 or 2 tablespoons very hot water to the can, stir with a fork, and add water and gravy to the dish you're making.

BEEF AND RICE CASSEROLE

One-dish Dinner

18 min.

- 1 #2 can cooked boiled rice
- 2 cups water
- 1 10-oz. can Italian spaghetti sauce, any style
- 1 tablespoon butter
- 2 teaspoons soy sauce
- ½ teaspoon chopped parsley
- ¼ teaspoon salt; pepper
- 1 12-oz. can roast beef
- bread crumbs mixed with a little grated cheese
- butter

Start broiler pre-heating to medium. Turn rice into water and place over highest heat. In another saucepan combine spaghetti sauce, butter, soy sauce, parsley, salt and a light dusting of pepper; place over medium heat. Break or cut meat into chunks. When rice boils, drain and add spaghetti sauce mixture; mix well, add meat, and combine. Taste and correct seasoning with salt and pepper. Cook 5 minutes, stirring occasionally, or until mixture is well heated. Turn into an ovenproof casserole; sprinkle top with bread crumbs and grated cheese, dot with butter, and brown under broiler.

Serves 6 to 8

THRIFTY SUBSTITUTE FOR ROAST BEEF

Hint

Try using canned corned beef when recipe calls for canned roast beef, especially where the meat is to be chopped. See Timesaver Index for a quick easy way to chop canned corned beef.

BEEF CAKES

15 to 18 min.

- 1 egg
- 1 teaspoon onion juice
- ½ can condensed cream of mushroom soup
- 1 12-oz. can roast beef
- ½ cup (or more) bread crumbs
- celery salt
- ¼ teaspoon salt; pepper
- ½ teaspoon chopped parsley

Break egg into mixing bowl, add onion juice and soup; beat lightly. Add meat and can gravy; crush meat with a fork (see Note below). Add bread crumbs and all other ingredients; combine. Mixture should be stiff; add more crumbs if needed. Drop by spoonfuls into a hot skillet containing plenty of butter; flatten tops; fry 5 minutes to a side or until nicely browned.

Serve topped with chili sauce. (May be made into hamburger-like cakes, if desired.)

Note: If roast beef appears "stringy," cut into slices across the grain before adding to mixture.

Makes 8 to 12

Hint

BEEF CAKES—ADVANCE PREPARATION

Prepare above mixture; cover tightly with waxed paper and store in refrigerator until wanted. To cook, shape into hamburger-like patties and fry until browned on both sides. Takes about 15 minutes. Serve topped with chili sauce.

20 min.

BROILED BEEF HASH

1 #2 can baby potatoes
1 12-oz. can roast beef
1 tablespoon onion juice
1 3-oz. can mushroom bits and pieces
½ teaspoon salt; pepper
½ cup chili sauce or more
butter

Start broiler pre-heating to hot. Drain potatoes, rinse in cold water, and crush with a fork. Add meat and break into small chunks. To gravy remaining in meat can add onion juice, mushrooms, mushroom liquid, salt and a light dusting of pepper; mix well; add to meat mixture and combine by tossing. Spread out in a pie tin or on a heatproof serving platter; spread top with chili sauce, dot generously with butter. Cook under broiler flame for 10 minutes or until heated through and nicely browned.

Serves 4 generously

CORNED BEEF AND CABBAGETTES

1½ cups water
1 12-oz. can corned beef
1 package frozen Brussels sprouts
1 #2 can boiled baby potatoes
½ cup cooked carrots
salt and pepper
butter

20 min.

Start water boiling over highest heat. Dice corned beef (see Timesaver Index). When water boils, add Brussels sprouts and meat, lower heat to medium, cover pot and cook as directed on vegetable package. When sprouts are barely tender, add potatoes drained and rinsed in cold water, and carrots. Continue cooking until sprouts are tender; taste broth and season rather highly with pepper and salt as needed. Add a small chunk of butter and serve in soup plates, spooning broth over each portion.

Serves 4 to 6

CORNED BEEF HASH I

One-dish Dinner

¼ cup sour cream
½ teaspoon onion juice
¼ teaspoon pepper
½ teaspoon celery salt
1 #2 can corned beef hash
softened butter

15 min.

Light broiler to pre-heat. Combine sour cream, onion juice, pepper and celery salt. Turn hash into a bowl, crumble into bits; add sour cream mixture and toss to combine. Spread hash thinly in a pie tin, spread with butter, and place under hot broiler flame 8 to 10 minutes or until browned. Top each portion with a sunnyside egg or two, if desired.

Serves 2 or 3

One-dish Dinner

18 min.

CORNED BEEF HASH II

1 #2 can baby boiled potatoes
2 tablespoons butter
1 tablespoon olive oil
1 12-oz. can corned beef
½ teaspoon onion juice
celery salt
½ cup sour cream
salt and pepper

Start broiler pre-heating to medium hot. Drain potatoes, rinse in cold water, halve or quarter them and turn into a hot skillet containing butter and olive oil. Cook over medium heat until potatoes brown slightly (about 5 minutes). Meanwhile chop corned beef (see Timesaver below). Stir onion juice and a generous shake of celery salt into sour cream. Turn meat into skillet, combine with potatoes, spread with sour cream mixture, dust lightly with salt and pepper and mix again. Taste and correct seasoning. Brown hash under broiler for a few minutes.

Serves 4 generously

Time-saver

TO CHOP CANNED MEAT QUICKLY

Remove contents of can in one piece. Stand meat on its end, and make lengthwise and crosswise cuts, to within a half-inch of the bottom. (The more cuts you make, the finer the chopped result). Turn meat on its side, hold firmly with your left hand, and slice across the cuts you've made. The thinner you slice, the finer the chopped result.

One-dish Dinner

18 min.

CORNED BEEF HASH AND SCRAMBLED EGG RING

Prepare Corned Beef Hash I or II (see above). When hash is ready for broiler, pile it around the edge of a heatproof serving dish. Leave center open. While hash is under broiler, prepare Scrambled Eggs (see Index). To serve: pile eggs in center of serving dish;

garnish with a sprinkle of parsley or a few slices of Pickled Beets (see Index) and serve.

Serves 4 to 6

CREAMED CHIPPED BEEF

8 min.

4 teaspoons flour
1 cup Vichysoisse soup
pepper
1 4-oz. jar chipped beef

Measure flour into saucepan, add 2 tablespoons soup, stir with a fork until smooth. Place over medium heat. Slowly add remainder of soup and a light dusting of pepper; stir constantly until smooth. Cook until it bubbles, stirring often. Meanwhile, open jar of beef and pull into shreds; rinse under running water and drain. When sauce is ready, add meat; simmer 2 minutes and serve.

Note: If you like chipped beef "swimming" in cream sauce, double the quantity of soup and flour.

Serves 4

HOW TO SHRED CHIPPED BEEF QUICKLY

Time-saver

Remove meat from jar and roll into a cigar. Cut across cigar to make very thin slices—the thinner the slices, the finer the shredding. Pull slices apart with your fingers.

CREAMED CHIPPED BEEF, SHORTCAKE STYLE

One-dish Dinner

⅔ cup milk
2 cups biscuit mix
1 teaspoon parsley
1 recipe Creamed Chipped Beef (see above)
1 #2 can peas and carrots
salt and pepper
butter
paprika

20 min.

Start oven pre-heating to hot. Mix milk with biscuit mix, add parsley, and make into biscuit dough. Drop egg-size spoonfuls onto greased pie tin; flatten tops slightly and bake as directed on package. Meanwhile prepare creamed chipped beef, add peas and carrots drained and rinsed. Taste and correct seasoning with salt and pepper; have mixture thoroughly heated. To serve: split biscuits; arrange bottoms edge to edge on serving dish. Pour meat mixture over; replace tops of biscuits, also edge to edge. Top each biscuit with a bit of butter; dust with a trace of paprika. Serve with a green salad and a cold fruit dessert.

Note: If you prefer to use frozen vegetables, start water boiling for vegetables before mixing biscuits. Cook as directed on package; drain; add to meat mixture.

Serves 4 to 6

15 min.

CHEESEBURGERS THAT *ARE*

(*Main Meat Dish*)

2 tablespoons butter
half a 5-oz. jar sharp cheese
a pinch of salt
1 can brown gravy style hamburgers

Start broiler pre-heating to medium. Mash butter, cheese, and salt together. Slice hamburgers in two horizontally, spread cut sides with cheese mixture and top each half with a little gravy from the can. Arrange in a pie tin, pour remaining gravy around, and cook under broiler for 6 to 8 minutes. When ready, put halves back together again. Spoon gravy over, and serve.

Note: For *real* sandwiches, use brown-and-serve rolls. And for a different flavor, try blue-cheese-flavor jar cheese.

Serves 4

CORNED BEEF HASH CHEESEBURGERS

18 min.

Start broiler pre-heating to medium hot. Prepare cheese mixture as in Cheeseburgers (see above). Remove both ends of a #2 can corned beef hash; push hash out in one piece. Cut into thick slices; place on a greased pie tin, top each slice with a little butter and cook under broiler 8 to 10 minutes. Remove, put a generous spoonful of butter-cheese mixture on each "burger," return to broiler. Cook until topping browns and bubbles—about 3 or 4 minutes.

Serves 4

CREAMED HAM AND EGGS

One-dish Dinner

- 1 package bakery corn muffins (6)
- 4 teaspoons flour
- 1 cup Vichysoisse soup
- ¼ teaspoon salt
- ½ teaspoon onion juice
- ½ pound boiled ham, sliced
- 6 to 8 eggs

20 min.

Start oven on medium low; place muffins on a pie tin and put in oven to heat. Measure flour into a saucepan; add 2 tablespoons soup, salt, and onion juice; stir until smooth. Place over medium heat and slowly stir in remainder of soup. Cook, stirring occasionally, until sauce bubbles (about 5 minutes). While sauce is cooking, cut ham into coarse bits; beat eggs and season as directed in Scrambled Eggs (see Index). Put skillet on to pre-heat. When sauce is ready, stir in ham and remove from heat. Scramble eggs. When barely done, remove skillet from heat. Remove muffins from oven and cut in halves; butter, if desired; arrange in a single layer on serving plate, reserving one half of one muffin. Spread eggs over muffins, pile creamed ham in center of eggs; sprinkle top of creamed mixture with reserved muffin, crumbled.

Timesaver: Omit Vichysoisse soup, flour, salt, and onion juice. For sauce use 1 can condensed cream of mushroom soup, thinned with a few tablespoons milk. Heat; add chopped ham. Prepare eggs and muffins as directed. Serve with jam or marmalade on the side.

Serves 4 to 6

18 min.

HAM AND MUSHROOMS DE LUXE

1 can condensed cream of mushroom soup
½ cup sour cream
1 6-oz. can mushrooms
1 teaspoon onion juice
1 tablespoon butter
2 cups or ½ pound cooked ham, coarsely chopped
salt and pepper
buttered bread crumbs
Roquefort style "jar" cheese

Start broiler pre-heating to medium hot. Combine soup, sour cream, mushrooms, onion juice and butter in a saucepan; place over medium heat. Cook and stir occasionally until heated through but do not boil. Meanwhile chop meat. When soup mixture is ready, add meat and combine; continue cooking for 2 or 3 minutes; taste and correct seasoning with salt and pepper. Turn into a heatproof serving dish. Sprinkle bread crumbs on top in shape of an X. Between the arms of the X dab on generous teaspoonfuls of the cheese. Brown about 4 inches away from broiler heat for about 5 minutes, or until done. If desired, garnish with fresh parsley or canned pimiento rings before serving.

Serves 6 to 8

BREAD CRUMBS AS YOU NEED THEM

Hint

If you use bread crumbs only occasionally, buy a loaf of unsliced white bread, cut into quarters, and leave it in your oven for 4 or 5 days to dry out (remove bread if you do any baking). Store in an ordinary brown paper bag. When you need crumbs grate off desired amount. The bread keeps indefinitely.

HAM SALAD

20 min.

- 2 cups or ½ pound cooked ham, coarsely chopped
- ½ cup chopped celery
- 1 cucumber, chopped
- ½ cup mayonnaise
- ⅓ cup sour cream
- 2 tablespoons chopped parsley
- ½ teaspoon each, celery seed and (optional) caraway seed
- salt and pepper

Have all ingredients chilled. Chop ham, turn into salad bowl and return to refrigerator. Coarsely chop celery and peeled cucumber (see Timesaver below) and add to ham. Combine all other ingredients into a dressing; taste and correct seasoning. Just before serving, pour dressing over meat and vegetables, toss lightly to combine, and serve at once on beds of crisp greens. Garnish with hard-cooked egg quarters or tomato slices.

Serves 4 to 6

TO CHOP CELERY QUICKLY

Time-saver

Cut the whole bunch of celery in two, slightly below where the leaves begin. (Save the tender light green leaves for salad makings or soup.) Hold celery under forcefully running cold water to rinse; shake vigorously to remove excess water. Hold bunch of celery in your left hand, and using a large, sharp knife, slice across the cut end. The thinner you make the "slices," the finer the "chopped" celery.

HAM SALAD SANDWICH FILLING

- 2 tablespoons mayonnaise
- 2 tablespoons sour cream
- ¼ teaspoon onion juice
- a pinch of salt
- 1 cup or ¼ pound cooked or leftover ham, coarsely chopped
- 2 tablespoons green pepper, coarsely chopped

10 min.

Stir mayonnaise, sour cream, onion juice and salt until well combined. Pour over ham and green pepper. Toss lightly to coat meat with dressing.

Note: This filling is also delicious when stuffed into tomatoes.

Makes 4 to 6

EASY MEAT SALADS

Time-saver

Substitute an equal amount of cold, diced, canned meat for chicken in Chicken Salad I or II (see Index). Canned hamburgers (not chilled) may also be used. Dip each hamburger in hot water for a moment to rinse off gravy; save the water and use it for another dish.

SAUSAGES, PIZZA STYLE

- 1 package (4) English muffins
- 1 8-oz. can spaghetti sauce, plain tomato style
- 1 8-oz. can breakfast sausages
- American cheese slices

15 min.

Start broiler pre-heating to hot. Split muffins and place under broiler to toast. Place spaghetti sauce over medium heat; in another pan start sausages heating in their broth and fat. When muffins are lightly toasted, spoon hot spaghetti sauce over them, reserving a little sauce. Top with sausages. Return to broiler until sausages brown (about 5 minutes). Remove from heat, spoon over remainder of sauce, top each with a slice of cheese, and put under broiler again until cheese melts and bubbles slightly.

Variation: Rolled or flat anchovy filets, drained of oil, may be used instead of sausages. Cook anchovies under broiler for a minute or two only.

Makes 8

VIENNA SAUSAGE BROIL

15 min.

- 2 large tomatoes
- butter
- salt and pepper
- 2 tablespoons olive oil
- 1 teaspoon onion juice
- 1 or 2 6-oz. cans Vienna sausage
- bread crumbs and grated cheese, mixed

Start broiler pre-heating to medium hot. Cut tomatoes into 6 thick slices and arrange on a buttered pie tin. Put a bit of butter on each, dust lightly with salt and pepper and place under broiler flame. Whisk olive oil and onion juice together, adding a speck of salt and pepper. Drain sausages and rinse in cold water; slice each the long way into three pieces. Put into oil mixture and toss lightly. Remove tomatoes from broiler. Dribble oil mixture generously over tomatoes, then top with sausages. Return to broiler, cook 5 minutes or until slightly brown on top. Remove from broiler again, sprinkle bread crumb-cheese mixture over, and brown for a minute or two under the broiler.

Serves 4 to 6

FRANKFURTERS AND EGGS

15 min.

- 2 tablespoons butter
- 1 12-oz. can frankfurters
- 6 or 8 eggs
- 2 tablespoons sour cream
- salt and pepper

Melt butter in a large skillet over medium low heat. Rinse frankfurters in cold water, cut into half-inch rounds; turn into skillet and cook 8 to 10 minutes, shaking pan occasionally. Meanwhile beat eggs with sour cream, adding light seasonings. Pour eggs over meat. Cook "pancake" style, or scramble eggs. Serve with mild prepared mustard on the side, for dunking.

Serves 4 to 6

18 min.

CHILI CON CARNE

2 1 lb. cans chili con carne
2 tablespoons butter
1 fresh tomato, chopped
1 teaspoon onion juice
1 teaspoon sweet paprika
1 teaspoon brown sugar
¼ cup chicken broth
chili powder as desired (up to 2 teaspoons for *red* hot)

Turn chili con carne into a saucepan and place over medium heat. Stir occasionally, until heated through. In another saucepan, melt butter, and add all remaining ingredients except chili powder; simmer 5 minutes over low heat. Add to chili, combine, taste and correct seasoning, adding chili powder as desired. Simmer 3 or 4 minutes and serve with hot French bread.

Serves 4 generously

One-dish Dinner

20 min.

CHOW MEIN (or Chop Suey)

2 cups water
¼ cup chicken broth
½ teaspoon onion juice
1 package frozen or 1 can Chow Mein or Chop Suey (see Note below)
½ cup Chinese bean sprouts
2 tablespoons butter
1 cup coarsely chopped celery
1 cup canned cooked rice
half a small head of lettuce
salt and pepper; soy sauce

Put water on to boil over highest heat. In another pan bring chicken broth to simmer, add onion juice and Chow Mein. *If frozen* cook one minute, turn block over and cook for another minute or so. Break into chunks with a knife point. *If canned,* drain off liquid. Add bean sprouts drained and rinsed, and simmer, stirring occasionally, until mixture is heated through. Melt butter in a large skillet and add chopped celery (see Timesaver Index). Cover and cook over medium low heat for about 10 minutes. Refresh rice in boiling water as directed on can; slice lettuce into shreds. To serve: turn chow mein mixture into skillet containing celery; combine, taste and correct seasoning with salt, pepper, and up to 1 teaspoon soy sauce. Keep hot. Make a mound of rice on a platter, dig a "well" in the center. Stir lettuce into chow mein, and immediately fill "well" in rice. Sprinkle top with chopped almonds, if desired, and serve at once.

Note: ½ cup or more drained, cleaned, cooked shrimp, chopped boned chicken, or chopped canned hamburgers without gravy, may be added to the skillet when adding Chow Mein.

1 package frozen or 1 can serves 2 or 3

Vegetables

ASPARAGUS, FROZEN CUTS

18 min.

"Frozen cuts" are pieces of tips and stems which are just as flavorful as the more expensive spears. Cook cuts by boiling, in just enough water to cover, for time directed on package. When tender, dress as for Asparagus, Frozen Spears (see below).

Serves 4

EVEN USE YOUR APRON-PUTTING-ON TIME

Time-saver

Before you do anything else in the kitchen, put vegetable water on to boil. By the time you're ready to start cooking, the water is boiling and you're that much ahead.

ASPARAGUS, FROZEN SPEARS

- 1 package frozen asparagus spears
- 1 teaspoon wine vinegar or lemon juice
- 2 tablespoons butter
- salt and pepper

18 min.

Cook asparagus in just enough water to cover for time directed on package. When tender, remove to a hot plate. Reserve ⅓ cup liquid, discard remainder. To liquid add vinegar or lemon juice, butter, and generous seasonings. Whisk to make a sauce. Pour over asparagus and serve at once.

Serves 4

20 min.

SKILLETED ASPARAGUS

2 tablespoons butter
2 teaspoons wine vinegar
2 tablespoons water
1 package frozen asparagus spears or cuts
salt and pepper

Melt butter in a heavy skillet. Add vinegar and water; whisk with a fork to blend. Place block of frozen asparagus in center of skillet; cover tightly and cook over low heat for 5 minutes, or until pieces can be separated. Increase heat slightly and start counting cooking time; cook as directed on package for boiling, or until tender. Keep pan covered and shake it frequently. Watch carefully. Serve with pan juices, seasoned with salt and pepper.

Serves 4

16 min.

SNAP BEANS, FROZEN

1 package frozen snap beans
1 tablespoon butter
½ teaspoon lemon juice
salt and pepper

Cook beans as directed on package. When just tender, add butter, lemon juice, and generous seasonings. Heat through and serve at once.

Serves 4

16 min.

SNAP BEANS AND HAM

Prepare Snap Beans, Frozen (see above). After seasoning, add 2 or 3 thin slices of boiled ham, coarsely chopped. Serve at once. If beans must stand a few minutes before serving, add ham just before bringing to the table.

Serves 4 to 6

SNAP BEANS, SPANISH STYLE (FROZEN)

18 min.

- 1 package "Frenched" frozen string beans
- ⅓ cup chili sauce
- tomato juice
- 1 tablespoon butter
- a pinch of sugar
- salt and pepper
- a pinch of chili powder

Cook string beans as directed on package, using chili sauce and tomato juice as liquid. Do not drain. When tender, add butter, season lightly with salt and pepper, add a pinch of sugar; add chili powder, if desired. Serve beans in sauce.

Serves 4

"FRENCHED" SNAP BEANS

Hint

These are cut in slivers instead of pieces, and seem to have a bit more flavor. Also, they cook in less time. Try them next time you buy snap beans.

TO KEEP THAWED FROZEN VEGETABLES

Hint

To preserve frozen vegetables which may thaw before you get a chance to serve them, cook in lightly salted water until barely done. Drain, and store in a covered dish. They will keep for 2 or 3 days in your refrigerator. To serve, reheat in butter, add a little cream, and season as desired.

SNAP BEANS IN CREAM

20 min.

- 1 package "Frenched" frozen snap beans
- 1 tablespoon butter
- 1 teaspoon flour
- 3 tablespoons heavy cream
- salt and pepper
- celery salt
- paprika

Cook beans as directed on package. When tender, drain, reserving about ¼ cup of the liquid. Turn beans into a hot dish and keep hot. Melt butter in bean pan over low heat, stir in flour; blend smooth; slowly add reserved bean liquid and cream; stir to make a thin smooth sauce. Season well, add beans, simmer a minute or two and serve lightly sprinkled with paprika.

Note: Chopped ham may also be added.

Serves 4

10 min.

LEFTOVER SNAP BEANS

2 teaspoons finely chopped onion
2 teaspoons butter
½ cup leftover snap beans
1 tablespoon light cream
1 tablespoon grated Parmesan cheese

(Increase quantities accordingly for greater amount of vegetable.)

Sauté onion in butter until soft and yellow, using a saucepan. Add beans, combine, heat through. Mix in cream, then cheese. Continue heating until cheese begins to melt.

Note: This is also an excellent way to serve canned snap beans, leftover peas, lima beans, etc.

Serves 2

10 min.

CANNED SNAP BEANS

2 tablespoons butter
1 thin slice onion
3 tablespoons cream
1 #2 can snap beans
salt and pepper

Simmer butter, onion, and cream for 5 minutes in a saucepan over low heat. Meanwhile drain beans and rinse in cold water. Discard onion, add beans, toss to coat with sauce. Taste and correct seasoning, heat through, and serve at once.

Serves 4 to 6

TO DRAIN AND RINSE CANNED VEGETABLES

Time-saver

Don't cut top off can completely; leave about ½ inch of metal to act as a hinge. Hold fingers over top, tip can over sink and drain. Bend top back a little, fill can with cold water, close top, and drain again. Repeat as needed. If vegetables are to be soaked in cold water, do it right in the can!

LIMA BEANS, FROZEN

20 min.

- 1 package frozen lima beans
- 1 tablespoon butter
- salt and pepper
- 1 teaspoon lemon juice
- a dash of paprika

Cook beans as directed on package. When tender, drain, add butter and generous seasonings. Add lemon juice and toss lightly to mix, being careful not to crush the beans. Finish with a dash of paprika. Serve at once.

Serves 4 to 6

TO KEEP COOKED VEGETABLES CRISP

Hint

Drain boiled vegetables as soon as tender, to avoid any sogginess. Season, cover, and set aside. Reheat over low heat, if necessary.

LIMA BEANS IN CREAM

18 min.

Follow ingredients and method for Snap Beans in Cream (see above). Cook for time indicated on lima bean package.

Serves 4

10 min.

CANNED GREEN LIMA BEANS

1 #2 can green lima beans
2 tablespoons heavy cream
1 tablespoon butter
chopped parsley
salt and pepper
celery salt
a pinch of sugar

Drain beans and rinse lightly in cold water. Simmer cream, butter and parsley for a minute or so; add beans, combine; taste and correct seasoning (being sparing with the sugar). Heat through and serve at once.

Serves 4 to 6

CANNED DRIED LIMA BEANS

15 min.

1 #2 can cooked dried lima beans
⅛ teaspoon baking soda
1 tablespoon hot water
1 tablespoon butter
½ cup chopped lean boiled ham
salt and pepper

Turn beans into a saucepan and place over medium low heat. Dissolve soda in hot water and add with butter and ham. Heat thoroughly; taste and correct seasoning with salt and pepper.

Note: Instead of ham, 6 slices of crisp crumbled bacon may be added at the last possible moment before serving.

Serves 4

20 min.

CANNED BAKED BEANS

2 or 3 slices raw bacon, chopped
salt
1 teaspoon onion juice
2 tablespoons chili sauce
a pinch of dry mustard
1 tablespoon dark molasses
1 #2 can baked beans

Cook bacon in a deep skillet over medium heat until it browns (takes 3 or 4 minutes). Drain off fat.

Sprinkle bacon with a few grains of salt. Add all other ingredients except beans, and mix; add beans and mix again. Cover pan and simmer 12 to 15 minutes over low heat.

Serves 4

SCORCH PROOF COOKING

Time-saver

If you're going to be so busy in the kitchen you won't have time to watch canned vegetables—turn them into a double boiler to heat. They *can't* scorch.

BUTTERED BEETS

10 min.

1 small onion, thinly sliced
1 tablespoon butter
2 tablespoons heavy cream
½ teaspoon lemon juice
1 #2 can sliced beets
salt and pepper

Sauté onion in butter for 3 minutes, using a saucepan. Discard onion, add cream and lemon juice. Whisk into a sauce, using a fork. Add beets and a few tablespoons of beet liquid (reserve remainder for Beet Soup or Pickled Beets [see Index]). Toss to coat beets with sauce, heat through, season lightly with salt and pepper and serve at once.

Serves 4 to 6

BEETS IN SOUR CREAM

15 min.

1 tablespoon butter
½ teaspoon onion juice
1 #2 can sliced beets
½ cup or less sour cream
salt and pepper

Melt butter in saucepan, whisk in onion juice. Add 3 tablespoons liquid from beets and sour cream; season generously with salt and pepper and mix. Drain beets (reserve the liquid for Beet Soup or Pickled Beets [see Index]) and combine with sour cream mixture. Keep over low heat until heated through; do not boil.

Serves 6 to 8

A THRIFTY BUY IN BEETS

Hint

Unless the recipe specifies otherwise, buy sliced beets. They're thriftier, and in taste differ in no way from "baby" or whole beets.

15 min.

PICKLED BEETS

1 #2 can whole baby beets
1 tablespoon brown sugar
⅓ cup wine vinegar
2 whole cloves
6 peppercorns
6 thin slices of onion
1 teaspoon salt

Add water to liquid from beets to make 1 cup, and simmer with sugar, vinegar, cloves and peppercorns for 5 minutes. Arrange layers of beets and onion rings in a jar or deep bowl and pour liquid over. Cover and store in refrigerator for a day or so before using.

Note: Make these in advance and keep on hand for a quick garnish, hors d'oeuvres or salad course.

Makes 6 to 12 servings

16 min.

BRUSSELS SPROUTS, FROZEN

1 package frozen Brussels sprouts
1 tablespoon butter
2 tablespoons sour cream (or sweet cream if desired)
salt and pepper

Cook sprouts by boiling as directed on package. In another pan, melt butter over low heat, add sour (or sweet) cream, and season rather highly with salt and pepper. Do not boil sauce. Drain sprouts, add to sauce, toss lightly, and serve at once.

Serves 4

SAUCE FOR CABBAGE

Hint

The sauce described for Brussels Sprouts (see above) is an unusual treat on boiled or steamed cabbage, especially if made with sour cream.

BRUSSELS SPROUTS AU GRATIN

20 min.

1 package frozen Brussels sprouts
1 tablespoon butter
1 teaspoon wine vinegar
salt and pepper
½ cup bread crumbs mixed with grated cheese
butter

Cook sprouts as directed on package. Drain, dress with melted butter, vinegar, salt and pepper whisked together (keep seasoning on the light side). Arrange the sauce-coated sprouts in a single layer on a pie tin or serving dish; sprinkle with bread crumb mixture and dot each sprout with a bit of butter; place under medium broiler heat until brown and bubbly on top—about 4 minutes. Serve at once.

Serves 4

CANNED CARROTS, LEMON STYLE

10 min.

1 #2 can carrots
1 tablespoon butter
tip of bayleaf
1 teaspoon lemon juice
1 teaspoon brown sugar
salt and pepper

Drain carrots, rinse in cold water and drain well. In a saucepan melt butter, add all ingredients except carrots, and whisk to mix. Simmer 2 or 3 minutes. Add carrots, toss to coat with sauce, heat through slowly. Taste and correct seasoning, adding a little more sugar if desired. Discard bayleaf and serve.

Serves 4 to 6

CANDIED CARROTS

10 to 15 min.

1 tablespoon butter
2 tablespoons honey
1 teaspoon lemon juice
1 #2 can carrots
salt and pepper
sweet paprika

Start broiler pre-heating to medium hot. Melt butter in a pie tin, add honey and lemon juice; mix. Drain carrots, rinse in cold water and drain well; turn into pie tin in an even layer and dust lightly with salt and pepper. Toss carrots to coat with sauce; sprinkle sparingly with paprika and place under broiler heat 6 to 10 minutes, or until faintly browned.

Serves 4 to 6

CAULIFLOWER, FROZEN

12 min.

1 package frozen cauliflower
1 tablespoon butter
pinch of grated nutmeg
2 tablespoons sour cream
¼ teaspoon salt
⅛ teaspoon pepper

Cook cauliflower as directed on package. Meanwhile melt butter in another pan, add all ingredients and whisk together to make a sauce. Keep over low heat (do not boil) until cauliflower is ready. Pour sauce over vegetable to serve.

Serves 4

VEGETABLES AU GRATIN

Hint

Before adding cheese, vegetables should be seasoned and coated with butter. Since cheese is slightly salty to the taste, be sparing of salt.

Cream Sauce (see Index) may be used as a binder for au gratin cookery. Sauce should be a little thicker than usual, and very hot when added to vegetable.

A good topping for au gratin dishes is grated mild cheese such as Swiss or Cheddar, mixed with an equal quantity of bread crumbs. A half cup of this mixture is ample for 1 package of frozen vegetables. When dotted with butter and browned under a hot broiler, this topping makes a rich brown crust. For sharper flavor, use sharp cheese.

For a smoother topping, use ¾ cup grated cheese and ¼ cup bread crumbs.

CAULIFLOWER AU GRATIN

20 min.

- 1 package frozen cauliflower
- 4 teaspoons flour
- 1 cup Vichysoisse soup
- ¼ teaspoon salt
- ¼ teaspoon onion juice
- salt and pepper
- ½ cup bread crumbs and grated cheese mixture

Start broiler pre-heating to medium. Start cauliflower cooking as directed on package. Measure flour into another saucepan; add 2 tablespoons soup, salt and onion juice. Stir until smooth; place over medium heat and slowly stir in remainder of soup. Cook, stirring occasionally until sauce bubbles. When cauliflower is ready season lightly with salt and pepper and pour sauce over, mix gently, and spread vegetable out in a pie tin. Sprinkle breadcrumb mixture over top and brown under broiler.

Timesaver: Cauliflower may also be prepared as directed in Brussels Sprouts Au Gratin (see Index).

Serves 4 to 6

SAVE SAUCE COOKING TIME

Time-saver

Whenever possible in vegetable cookery (as in the frozen cauliflower recipe above, for example) make the sauce in another pan while the vegetable is cooking. Just pour the sauce over the drained vegetable and you're ready to serve.

Note: Some stores sell "melted butter servers"—miniature saucepans, really, made of tin-lined copper. These are ideal for cooking vegetable sauces, since you can take the utensil right to the table and let people help themselves. Just sprinkle a little salt and pepper over the vegetable.

10 min.

CUT CORN, FROZEN

1 package frozen cut corn
2 tablespoons butter
1 teaspoon lemon juice
salt and pepper

Cook corn according to package directions, using barely enough water to cover. Drain, add butter, lemon juice, a light sprinkle of salt and pepper. Toss to combine and serve at once.

Serves 4

12 to 15 min.

SKILLETED CUT CORN

2 tablespoons butter
1 package frozen cut corn
1 teaspoon lemon juice
salt and pepper

Melt butter in a heavy skillet, add corn. (If in a solid block, cook over medium heat for a minute, turn block over and cook another minute or so. Break block into bits, using a fork; then start counting cooking time). Cover skillet closely and cook over low heat for time directed on package. Add lemon juice and a light dusting of salt and pepper, combine, and serve with pan juices.

Serves 4

CUT CORN, CANNED

10 min.

1 #2 can kernel style corn
1 tablespoon butter
1 thin slice onion
2 tablespoons tomato juice
1 tablespoon cream
salt and pepper

Drain and rinse corn. Melt butter in a saucepan, add onion, simmer a few minutes; discard onion, add tomato juice, cream, and a light sprinkling of salt and pepper. Whisk sauce with a fork to combine. Add corn, toss to coat kernels, and heat through before serving.

Serves 4

CREAM STYLE CORN

10 min.

1 #2 can cream style corn
1 tablespoon butter
¼ teaspoon celery salt
2 tablespoons sour cream
⅛ teaspoon pepper

Combine all ingredients and heat slowly over low heat. When butter is melted, stir it through the corn. Simmer a minute or two more, and serve. Do not boil.

Serves 4

QUICK-COOKING FROZEN VEGETABLES

Time-saver

Frozen vegetables cook in less time if the block is broken into chunks before putting into boiling water. Cut leaf vegetables, like spinach, into quarters, using a sharp pointed knife. Seed vegetables, like peas, corn, or beans break apart easily if you nudge them with a fork after putting into the water.

18 min.

SUCCOTASH, FROZEN OR CANNED

1 package frozen succotash
1 tablespoon butter
2 tablespoons cream
a pinch of brown sugar
¼ teaspoon salt
pepper
2 thin slices boiled ham

Cook frozen succotash as directed on package. In another saucepan melt butter, add cream, sugar, salt and a generous dusting of pepper; combine and simmer over low heat until vegetable is ready. Add sauce, toss to combine, taste and correct seasoning with salt. Just before serving add ham and toss again.

Canned Succotash: Heat through over low heat, adding butter and cream. Taste and correct seasoning with sugar, salt, and pepper.

Serves 4 to 6

SUCCOTASH FROM LEFTOVER CORN AND BEANS

One cup serves 2. If vegetables are raw, cook together. Start beans and cook about 10 minutes before adding corn. Season as directed in Succotash recipe above. If vegetables are cooked, combine and heat; add a little brown sugar and cream. Be careful not to overseason.

10 to 15 min.

BROILED ONIONS

1 #2 can boiled onions ("baby" variety preferred)
2 tablespoons butter
salt and pepper
paprika

Drain and rinse onions with cold water. Melt butter in a pie tin, roll onions in the butter, being careful not to crush them. Dust lightly with salt, generously with pepper; sprinkle a little paprika over and brown under the broiler (5 to 10 minutes).

Serves 4 to 6

CREAMED ONIONS

12 min.

4 teaspoons flour
1 cup Vichysoisse soup
¼ teaspoon salt
pepper

1 #2 can boiled onions ("baby" variety preferred)
2 tablespoons sour cream
paprika

Measure flour into a saucepan; add 2 tablespoons soup, salt, and a light dusting of pepper; stir until smooth. Place over medium heat and slowly stir in remainder of soup. Cook, stirring occasionally, until sauce bubbles (about 5 minutes). Drain and rinse onions; add to sauce and simmer slowly for 5 minutes. Just before serving, stir in sour cream. Dust top lightly with paprika.

Serves 4 to 6

ONIONS AU GRATIN

18 min.

Prepare Creamed Onions (see above). Spread onions out in a pie tin and sprinkle with bread crumb-grated cheese mixture. Brown under a hot broiler heat. Or, prepare Broiled Onions (see above). Before placing under broiler sprinkle onions generously with ½ cup bread crumbs mixed with grated cheese. Omit paprika.

Serves 4 to 6

CANNED VEGETABLE "BARGAINS"

Hint

Play it safe when you see a sale of a vegetable whose brand you're not familiar with. Buy one can; take it home and try it. If you like the quality, stock up.

10 min.

PEAS, FROZEN
(*or Frozen Peas and Carrots*)

1 package frozen peas
2 tablespoons butter
1 tablespoon heavy cream
a tiny pinch of nutmeg
salt and pepper

Cook peas as directed on package. When tender, drain, add butter, cream, nutmeg, and a light dusting of salt and pepper. Toss gently and serve at once.

Serves 4

FROZEN PEAS DE LUXE

15 min.

2 tablespoons butter
1 teaspoon flour
½ cup water
1 package frozen peas
3 lettuce leaves, shredded
1 teaspoon onion juice
salt and pepper

Melt butter in a large saucepan. Measure flour into mixing bowl, add butter and stir into a paste. Measure water into same saucepan and place over high heat; add peas. When thawed, add lettuce, onion juice, and ¼ teaspoon salt; stir once or twice. When water boils, reduce heat and cook 6 minutes or until peas are tender. Drain cooking water slowly into bowl containing flour-butter mixture, stirring constantly to make a smooth sauce. Add sauce to peas, combine, taste and correct seasoning and serve at once.

Note: Up to 1 cup shredded lettuce may be added, if desired.

Serves 4 to 6

FROZEN FOODS—COOKING TIME

Hint

Don't suspect the comparatively short cooking times printed on frozen vegetable packages. For best results, follow them to the minute. Frozen vegetables are partly "cooked" as part of the freezing process—enough to reduce greatly the time needed for just right doneness.

Don't overcook vegetables; drain cooking water away as soon as they are done.

CANNED PEAS

10 min.

1 #2 can peas
cold water
2 tablespoons butter
1 thin slice onion
¼ teaspoon sugar
¼ teaspoon salt
2 tablespoons cream

Drain peas and turn into a bowl filled with cold water. Soak for 2 or 3 minutes and drain well. Meanwhile, in a saucepan melt butter, add onion, sugar, and salt. Simmer 3 or 4 minutes, discard onion, add peas and cream. Toss gently. Heat through and serve at once.

Serves 4

CANNED PEAS AND CARROTS

10 min.

Drain and rinse one #2 can peas and carrots. Prepare as for Canned Peas (see above) or Lemon Style Carrots (see Index).

For leftovers: combine approximately equal parts of cooked peas and carrots. If not previously seasoned, prepare as for Canned Carrots, Lemon Style. Or, if seasoned, add 1 tablespoon cream while heating.

Serves 4

CANNED-VEGETABLE SEASONING

Hint

When that just-right fullness of flavor seems to elude you as you season canned vegetables, try adding a tiny pinch of sugar.

CANNED BOILED POTATOES

1 #2 can boiled potatoes
water
2 teaspoons onion juice
¼ teaspoon pepper
1 teaspoon salt
melted butter
chopped parsley

10 min.

Drain and rinse potatoes; turn into a saucepan and add just enough water to cover. Add onion juice, pepper, and salt; place over high heat until water boils. Simmer 5 minutes, or until heated through. Drain. To serve: roll potatoes in melted butter; sprinkle lightly with salt and pepper. For parsley potatoes, add 1 teaspoon or more chopped parsley to butter for potatoes.

Note: "Baby" potatoes heat through in about 5 minutes; allow more time for larger potatoes, or, to *save* time, halve or quarter larger potatoes.

Serves 4

WAXED PAPER "WASTE PAPER"

Time-saver

Peel vegetables like potatoes or onions, or do other waste-producing kitchen work over a sheet of waxed paper. When you're through, roll up the paper and toss it in the trash—and your working surfaces are clean and dry.

10 min.

TEN-MINUTE BOILED POTATOES

3 cups water
½ teaspoon salt
2 teaspoons onion juice
¼ teaspoon pepper
4 medium-size potatoes

Start water boiling over highest heat, adding salt, onion juice, and pepper. Peel potatoes and cut into half-inch cubes. Turn into water and cook for 6 minutes over highest heat, or until tender. Drain and serve as for Canned Boiled Potatoes (see above).

Serves 4

POTATOES WITH ONIONS

Hint

If you don't know this potato-cookery secret, try it. You won't taste the onion, as used in the following recipes—but your potatoes will taste far *more* like potatoes than if cooked the ordinary way.

Sour cream in mashed potatoes is another seasoning trick to try. You can't taste the cream—just a good, savory richness!

DON'T BOIL TOO MUCH WATER

Time-saver

When the recipe calls for a certain amount of water, measure it! Judging by eye means you err on the generous side, to be safe. Obviously, it takes more time to bring two cups of water to a boil than one.

CREAMED POTATOES I

15 min.

1 #2 can boiled potatoes
2 teaspoons onion juice
¼ teaspoon pepper
1 teaspoon salt
¼ cup light cream
butter

Drain and rinse potatoes; turn into a saucepan and barely cover with water. Add onion juice, pepper, and salt. Place over highest heat until water boils; simmer 5 minutes. Drain, reserving 2 tablespoons liquid. Remove and mash 1 medium-size or 3 baby-size potatoes; add reserved liquid and cream, combine, and add to potatoes in pan. Add a generous chunk of butter. Place over low heat and simmer, stirring occasionally, for 4 or 5 minutes. Taste and correct seasoning with salt and pepper before serving.

Note: If potatoes are large, dice, or cut in halves or quarters.

Serves 4 to 6

CREAMED POTATOES II

3 cups water
salt
onion juice
1/4 teaspoon pepper
4 medium-size potatoes
1 cup Vichysoisse soup
4 teaspoons flour
butter

18 min.

Start water boiling over highest heat, adding 1/2 teaspoon salt, 2 teaspoons onion juice, and pepper. Add potatoes, peeled and cut into half-inch cubes. Cook 6 minutes over high heat or until tender. Meanwhile measure 1/4 cup Vichysoisse soup into another saucepan; add flour, 1/4 teaspoon onion juice, and a pinch of salt. Stir until smooth. Place over medium heat and slowly add remainder of soup, stirring constantly. Cook, stirring occasionally, until sauce bubbles (about 5 minutes). If ready before potatoes are tender, remove from heat. Drain potatoes, add to sauce with a generous chunk of butter. Combine, taste and correct seasoning with salt and pepper; simmer over low heat, stirring occasionally, for 5 minutes.

Serves 4 to 6

4 min.

FOUR-MINUTE FRIED POTATOES

1 #2 can cocktail shoestring potatoes
3 tablespoons butter
salt and pepper

Melt butter in a skillet over low heat. Add potatoes and shake skillet vigorously. Heat for two minutes by the clock. Taste and season carefully with salt and pepper (potatoes already contain some seasoning). Serve at once.

Serves 3 or 4

FRIED POTATOES, HOME STYLE

15 min.

1 #2 can boiled potatoes
2 tablespoons butter
1 teaspoon onion juice
salt and pepper

Drain, rinse, and slice potatoes. Melt butter in a heavy skillet over medium heat, add onion juice and whisk to combine. Add potatoes and sprinkle lightly with salt and pepper. Cook over medium heat, shaking skillet frequently, until nicely browned.

Serves 4 to 6

FIVE-MINUTE HASHED CREAMED POTATOES

5 min.

3 tablespoons butter
1 #2 can cocktail shoestring potatoes
3 tablespoons heavy cream
salt and pepper

Melt butter in a skillet over low heat. Add potatoes and shake skillet vigorously. Heat for 2 minutes by the clock, add cream and shake skillet again. Cook one more minute, adjust seasoning, and serve at once.

Serves 3 or 4

POTATOES HASHED IN CREAM

20 min.

1 #2 can boiled potatoes
2 tablespoons butter
1 teaspoon onion juice
salt and pepper
4 to 6 tablespoons heavy cream

Drain, rinse, and dice potatoes. Melt butter in a heavy skillet over medium heat, add onion juice, and whisk to combine. Add potatoes and sprinkle lightly with salt and pepper. When faintly brown, add cream and continue cooking until nicely browned.

Serves 4 to 6

BROILER-BROWNED POTATOES

3 cups water
½ teaspoon salt
2 teaspoons onion juice
¼ teaspoon pepper
1 #2 can boiled baby potatoes
2 tablespoons butter

10 min.

Start water boiling over highest heat, adding salt, onion juice, and pepper. Drain and rinse potatoes and turn into water. When it boils, drain. Add butter and toss lightly to coat. Turn into a pie tin and place under medium broiler heat until lightly browned (about 5 minutes).

Serves 4 to 6

MASHED POTATOES

3 cups water
½ teaspoon salt
2 teaspoons onion juice
¼ teaspoon pepper
4 medium-size potatoes
2 tablespoons butter
2 tablespoons sour cream or light cream
celery salt

15 to 18 min.

Start water boiling over highest heat, adding salt, onion juice, and pepper. Peel potatoes and cut into half-inch cubes. Turn into water and cook for 6 minutes over highest heat, or until tender. Drain. Mash. Add butter and cream and a generous dash of celery salt. Beat with a rotary beater until light and fluffy; taste and correct seasoning with salt and pepper.

Timesaver: Use canned boiled baby potatoes, drained, rinsed, and halved. Turn into water. When it boils, drain and mash potatoes.

Serves 4 to 6

POTATO PATTIES

1 cup seasoned leftover mashed potatoes
1 egg yolk, lightly beaten
1 teaspoon chopped parsley
bread crumbs, if needed
butter
(For 1½ cups potatoes or more, use 1 whole egg)

Beat potatoes and egg together until smooth, adding parsley. If mixture is quite moist, add up to ¼ cup bread crumbs. Shape into patties and fry on both sides until brown in a hot skillet containing a generous lump of butter.

15 min.

Timesaver: Start broiler pre-heating to hot. Prepare potato mixture as directed. Form into walnut-size balls. Arrange in a buttered pie tin and flatten tops slightly. Push a bit of butter down into the top of each ball. Place under broiler until nicely browned (5 to 8 minutes).

1 cup mashed potatoes makes 3 or 4 patties

SAVE COOKING NEXT DAY'S POTATOES

Time-saver

When making mashed potatoes, double the recipe, and put half away in the refrigerator to use for patties the next day. Before storing, beat in egg as directed in Potato Patties (above); next night just shape patties and brown.

Note: To keep mashed potatoes best, turn into a bowl and push waxed paper down onto the surface of the potatoes so that it makes a tight fit all over.

BAKED SWEET POTATOES

20 min.

2 tablespoons butter
1 #2 can sweet potatoes
salt and pepper
paprika
brown sugar

Start oven pre-heating to hot. Melt butter in pie tin. Remove potatoes from can without crushing and roll in melted butter. Dust very lightly with salt and pepper, then paprika. Sprinkle a little brown sugar over each potato. Place in oven for 12 to 16 minutes, or until lightly browned.

Timesaver: Potatoes may be heated and browned under a medium broiler (5 to 7 minutes).

Serves 4 to 6

20 min.

MASHED SWEET POTATOES

3 cups water
¼ teaspoon salt
1 #2 can sweet potatoes
2 tablespoons butter
2 tablespoons heavy cream
a pinch of nutmeg
salt and pepper
celery salt

Start water boiling, adding salt. Add potatoes and simmer 5 minutes. Drain well, add butter, cream, and nutmeg. Mash and beat with a rotary beater; taste and correct seasoning with salt and pepper. Serve with a dash of celery salt on each portion, topped with a bit of butter.

Serves 4 to 6

12 to 15 min.

SWEET POTATO PATTIES I

1 egg, beaten
1 #2 can sweet potatoes
salt and pepper
1 teaspoon brown sugar
2 tablespoons butter
bread crumbs, if needed

Add egg to potatoes. Season lightly with salt and pepper, add sugar. Mash and beat with a rotary beater. Drop from a spoon into hot skillet containing butter. Flatten tops slightly and cook over medium heat 4 to 6 minutes to a side, or until nicely browned. If mixture is too moist to handle easily, add up to ¼ cup bread crumbs.

Serves 4 to 6

SWEET POTATO PATTIES II

1 cup seasoned leftover mashed sweet potatoes
1 egg yolk, lightly beaten
1 tablespoon cream
bread crumbs, if needed
butter

(For 1½ cups potatoes or more, use one whole egg.)

15 min.

Combine all ingredients except bread crumbs and beat smooth. If mixture is too moist to handle easily, add up to ¼ cup bread crumbs. Fry in plenty of butter in a hot skillet until nicely browned on both sides. Or use Timesaver method in Potato Patties, above.

1 cup mashed potatoes makes 3 or 4 patties

SPINACH, FROZEN

12 to 15 min.

1 package frozen spinach
1 tablespoon butter
1 tablespoon sour cream (sweet cream may be used)
salt and pepper

See package for amount of water; start it boiling. Cut block of spinach into quarters, turn into boiling water and cook as directed. When tender, drain, add butter, cream, and generous seasonings. Toss to combine and serve in individual dishes so that each person gets his share of the sauce.

Note: For quickest cooking buy chopped, rather than leaf spinach.

Serves 4

CREAMED SPINACH

14 min.

1 package frozen leaf spinach
4 teaspoons flour
1 cup Vichysoisse soup
¼ teaspoon salt
¼ teaspoon onion juice
salt and pepper

Cook spinach as directed on package. Meanwhile measure flour into another saucepan, add ¼ cup

Vichysoisse soup, salt, and onion juice. Stir until smooth. Place over medium heat and slowly stir in remainder of soup. Cook, stirring occasionally, until sauce bubbles (about 5 minutes). Remove from heat until spinach is ready. To serve: drain spinach, add to sauce and mix; taste and correct seasoning with salt and pepper; heat thoroughly and serve.

Serves 4 to 6

15 min.

CANNED SPINACH

1 #2 can spinach
1 tablespoon butter
1 thin slice onion
2 tablespoons light cream
celery salt
bayleaf tip
sour cream, if desired

Drain liquid from spinach and soak vegetable in cold water for 2 minutes. Drain and soak for another 2 minutes. Meanwhile melt 1 tablespoon butter in a saucepan, add onion, cream, a generous dash of celery salt and bayleaf. Simmer 5 minutes, discard onion and bayleaf. Add well-drained spinach, toss to coat with sauce, heat through slowly and serve. May be topped with sour cream.

Serves 4 to 6

16 min.

STEWED TOMATOES

2 tablespoons butter
⅓ cup bread crumbs (see Note below)
1 #2 can stewed tomatoes, whole-pack or regular
½ teaspoon onion juice
½ teaspoon salt
½ teaspoon sugar
celery salt; pepper

Melt butter in a pie tin, stir in bread crumbs and place under a medium broiler to toast. Stir occasionally. Meanwhile bring tomatoes, onion juice, salt, and sugar to a boil over highest heat; reduce heat and simmer 10 minutes. Taste and correct seasoning, adding a dash of celery salt and pepper. Just before serving stir in bread crumbs.

Note: For thicker Stewed Tomatoes, use ½ cup or more bread crumbs.

Serves 6 to 8

MIXED VEGETABLES

Frozen or canned, these are real time (and work!) savers for soups, or meat, fowl, and fish dishes. And, of course, mixed vegetables are delicious in their own right.

Time-saver

To cook frozen mixed vegetables, follow time on package. Season as directed for Peas, Frozen (see Index). Prepare canned mixed vegetables as for Canned Snap Beans or Canned Carrots, Lemon Style (see Index).

Sauces and Gravies

Canned Soups Used as Sauces

MUSHROOM OR CELERY SAUCE

10 min.

For Fish, Croquettes, Casserole Dishes:

garlic clove
1 teaspoon butter
½ teaspoon onion juice
⅓ cup milk
½ teaspoon Worcestershire sauce
1 can condensed cream of mushroom or celery soup

Rub a saucepan lightly with garlic. Add butter and onion juice; simmer 3 minutes. Add milk, Worcestershire sauce and soup; stir until smooth. Do not boil; sauce is ready when soup is heated through. For thinner sauce, add more milk.

Makes about 2 cups of sauce

TOMATO SAUCE

10 min.

For Fish, Croquettes, Casserole Dishes, Meats, Farinaceous foods:

¼ cup plain chicken broth
1 teaspoon tomato paste
½ teaspoon Worcestershire sauce
1 teaspoon chopped parsley
¼ teaspoon onion juice
1 can condensed tomato soup

Combine all ingredients in a saucepan. Heat through over low heat; simmer 2 or 3 minutes and sauce is ready. For thinner sauce, add more broth.

Makes about 2 cups of sauce

VEGETABLE SAUCE

8 min.

For Meats, Steamed or Poached Fish:

- 1 can condensed vegetarian vegetable soup
- ⅓ cup tomato sauce
- ½ teaspoon onion juice
- 1 teaspoon butter
- 1 teaspoon soy sauce
- ¼ cup chicken broth

Combine all ingredients in a saucepan and simmer 5 minutes.

Makes about 2 cups of sauce

QUICK RICH CREAM SAUCE

8 min.

For two	*For four*
1 cup Vichysoisse soup	2 cups Vichysoisse soup
4 teaspoons flour	3 scant tablespoons flour
¼ teaspoon salt	½ teaspoon salt
½ teaspoon onion juice	1 teaspoon onion juice

Measure flour into a saucepan, add from 2 to 4 tablespoons soup, salt, and onion juice; stir until smooth. Place over medium heat and slowly stir in remainder of soup. Cook, stirring occasionally, until sauce bubbles. Remove from heat if not to be used immediately.

For 2 or 4 servings

SAVE THE EXTRA SOUP

Hint

Pour soup left over from sauce-making into a glass jar; cover tightly and store in refrigerator. It will keep well for 2 to 4 days, depending on your refrigerator.

RICH CREAM SAUCE

12 min.

2 tablespoons butter
2 tablespoons flour
1 cup chicken broth
salt and pepper

optional:
1 teaspoon onion juice
½ teaspoon Worcestershire sauce

Melt butter in a saucepan over low heat; add flour and stir until smooth. Add a few tablespoons broth, stir smooth, add remainder of broth slowly, stirring constantly. Add optional ingredients; taste and correct seasoning with salt and pepper. Cook over low heat, stirring occasionally, 5 to 7 minutes.

Makes about 1 cup

SHARP SAUCE

12 min.

Prepare Rich Cream Sauce (above), adding optional ingredients and ½ to 1 teaspoon prepared mustard. Use the dark brown variety of mustard for more flavor.

Makes about 1 cup

BLAND CREAM SAUCE

12 min.

2 tablespoons butter
2 tablespoons flour
1 cup milk, or half milk and half light cream
⅛ teaspoon dry mustard
¼ teaspoon celery salt
salt and pepper

Melt butter in a saucepan over low heat. Add flour and stir until smooth. Add a few tablespoons milk, stir smooth, add remainder of milk very slowly, stirring constantly. Add seasonings; taste and correct flavor with salt and pepper. Cook over very low heat, stirring occasionally, 5 to 7 minutes.

Note: Some cooks prefer to scald milk or cream

before using in a cream sauce. If *you* do, use regular milk rather than homogenized, which sometimes clots when heated.

Makes about 1 cup

18 min.

CHEESE SAUCE

Prepare Bland Cream Sauce (above). After adding all the milk and correcting the seasoning, add 1/4 pound or more American, Swiss, Gruyere or packaged process cheese. Cook, stirring occasionally, over low heat until cheese melts and sauce is smooth.

Note: For a slightly heightened flavor, increase mustard to 1/4 teaspoon.

Makes about 1½ cups

Hint

HERBS IN SAUCES

Sauces with sprightly flavors are simple to make when you use herbs as the seasoning agent. You don't have to be an "expert" cook to use herbs with success, nor do you need a large and exotic collection. A few everyday varieties will serve you well for most any cooking: tarragon, fennel, chervil, dill, dried celery leaves or celery seeds, and, of course, parsley.

Sauces for Fish

Easiest of all fish dishes to make call for poaching, steaming, or broiling filets, and serving coated with a sauce, or with a sauce on the side.

The following sauces are for any fish having a delicate flavor, like flounder, haddock, cod, or salmon, all of which are usually available frozen at your grocers. Or use fresh filets.

To serve attractively, arrange the cooked filets on a heatproof platter and pour the sauce over; if desired, sprinkle fish with a few bread crumbs, dot with butter and brown for a moment or two under the broiler. Remember that too much heat destroys delicate herb flavors.

FENNEL SAUCE

5 min.

- garlic
- 1/8 teaspoon ground fennel
- a pinch each of tarragon and chervil
- 2 tablespoons softened butter

Cut off a bit of garlic about as big as a match head and crush to a paste. Add herbs and butter; mix well. Spread on hot fish just before serving.

Serves 4

LEMON SAUCE

5 min.

- 3 tablespoons butter
- a generous pinch of tarragon
- a tiny pinch of nutmeg
- 4 teaspoons lemon juice

Melt butter over hot water and whisk in other ingredients. Keep over hot water for a minute or two, whisk again and spread over hot fish.

Serves 4

SHERRY SAUCE

5 min.

- 3 tablespoons butter
- 1/2 teaspoon lemon juice
- 1/4 teaspoon salt
- 1/4 cup dry sherry
- a very tiny pinch ground fennel

Melt butter in a saucepan. Add all ingredients except fennel, bring to a quick simmer and cook 3 minutes over low heat. Add fennel, whisk to combine and spoon over very hot fish.

Serves 4

8 min.

DILL SAUCE

2 tablespoons butter
2 teaspoons heavy cream
¼ teaspoon ground dill
tiny pinch each of tarragon and chervil
a thin slice of garlic

Melt butter over hot water. Add all ingredients and whisk together. Keep over hot water for 5 minutes, stirring occasionally. Discard garlic, and spoon over very hot fish.

Serves 4

12 min.

HORSERADISH SAUCE

1 recipe Bland Cream Sauce (see Index)
2 tablespoons or less grated horseradish
1 egg yolk
2 tablespoons cream

Prepare sauce as directed, adding horseradish after it is ready. Mix well. Measure 3 or 4 tablespoons of the hot sauce into a cup. Slowly stir in egg yolk lightly beaten with cream. Mix well, and slowly pour egg mixture into sauce, stirring constantly. Merely heat through for a minute or two; do not boil. Pour over very hot fish, or serve on the side in a warmed dish.

Serves 4 to 6

10 min.

SOUR CREAM SAUCE

1 tablespoon butter
½ teaspoon onion juice
a thin sliver of garlic
½ cup sour cream
½ teaspoon salt
¼ teaspoon pepper
1 teaspoon chopped parsley

Melt butter in a small saucepan, add onion juice and garlic. Simmer a minute or two and discard garlic. Add sour cream, salt, pepper, and parsley. Combine; cook over low heat for 3 or 4 minutes but do not boil. When sauce is piping hot, serve at once.

Serves 4 to 6

Sauces for Meats

A rich, heartily flavored sauce is almost a "must" accompaniment to patties, hashes, etc. Always use the liquid packed in prepared meats as part of the sauce you're making, unless the recipe for the meat dish states otherwise.

MUSHROOM SAUCE

10 min.

- 3 tablespoons butter
- 1 3-oz. can mushroom pieces
- 1 3-oz. can mushroom caps
- 1 teaspoon onion juice
- 1 teaspoon soy sauce
- ½ cup liquid from meat or chicken, or can liquid plus water to make ½ cup; or ½ cup chicken broth
- salt and pepper

Melt butter in a saucepan. Add all ingredients except mushrooms, but include mushroom can liquid. Bring to a quick simmer and cook 5 minutes. Taste and correct seasoning with salt and pepper, add mushrooms, heat through, and serve. If desired, thicken sauce slightly with 1 teaspoon flour creamed with 1 teaspoon butter.

Serves 4 to 6

18 min.

ONION SAUCE

1 cup chicken broth
1 cup canned baby onions
2 tablespoons butter
2 tablespoons flour
1 teaspoon kitchen bouquet
½ teaspoon Worcestershire sauce
¼ teaspoon salt
dash of pepper
2 tablespoons sour cream

Start chicken broth heating over medium heat. Drain and rinse onions and turn into a skillet in which the butter has been melted. Cook over medium heat until onions begin to brown (about 5 minutes). Blend in flour and slowly add hot broth, stirring constantly until smooth. Stir in remaining ingredients except sour cream; mix well, taste and correct seasoning and simmer 5 minutes over low heat. Just before serving, stir in sour cream. Do not boil sauce after adding sour cream.

Serves 4 to 6

12 min.

QUICK ONION SAUCE

Prepare sauce as directed in recipe for Minute Steaks with Onion Sauce (see Index) using dehydrated onion soup.

Serves 4

5 min.

BARBECUE SAUCE

See recipe for Barbecued Hamburgers (Index). Prepare sauce as directed. If pan juices are not available, add ½ cup beef bouillon and 1 teaspoon kitchen bouquet to sauce.

Serves 3 or 4

QUICK CREOLE SAUCE

7 min.

- 2 tablespoons butter
- 1 #2 can "rice dinner" or Spanish or Creole rice
- 1 teaspoon soy sauce
- salt and pepper
- chicken broth, if needed

Melt butter in a saucepan over low heat. Add can of rice mixture and soy sauce. Beat vigorously with a rotary beater until smooth and the rice is well broken up. If sauce is too thick for your taste, thin with a little chicken broth. Taste and correct seasoning with salt and pepper; heat through and serve.

Serves 4 to 6

CONSOMMÉ, CHICKEN BROTH, OR BOUILLON FOR SAUCE COOKERY?

Hint

Each is a soup by itself, hence each has its own flavor. Consommé or bouillon may be used instead of chicken broth in making sauces, but the finished product will have the characteristic taste of the substitution. The delicate flavor of whatever meat, fowl, or fish you're serving might then be overpowered. So for best results, use plain chicken broth. Keep a supply of the canned product on your shelf.

ITALIAN SAUCE, MEAT STYLE

20 min.

- 1 tablespoon olive oil
- 1 garlic clove, split
- 1 package frozen chopped beef (or ½ pound fresh)
- 1 10-oz. can Italian sauce, meat style (if concentrated, do not dilute)
- 1 8-oz. can tomato sauce
- 1 teaspoon soy sauce
- 1 teaspoon onion juice
- bayleaf tip
- salt and pepper
- 1 3-oz. can mushrooms, if desired

Measure oil into saucepan; add garlic and meat. Cook over medium high heat, turning meat often and breaking cakes (or fresh meat) into pea-size bits as fast as possible (use a fork). Discard garlic, add all other ingredients. Simmer 10 to 12 minutes over medium low heat, stirring occasionally. Taste and correct seasoning with salt and pepper before serving.

Serves 4

15 min.

QUICK ITALIAN SAUCE, MEAT STYLE

- 1 tablespoon olive oil
- 1 garlic clove, split
- 1 10-oz. can Italian sauce, meat style (if concentrated, do not dilute)
- 1 can hamburgers, tomato sauce style
- 1 8-oz. can tomato sauce
- 1 teaspoon soy sauce
- 1 teaspoon onion juice
- bayleaf tip
- salt and pepper

Heat oil in a skillet, add garlic and cook 1 minute. Discard garlic, add hamburgers and can gravy. Crush meat with a fork and add all other ingredients. Simmer 10 to 12 minutes over medium low heat, stirring occasionally. Taste and correct seasoning with salt and pepper before serving.

Serves 4

20 min.

ITALIAN SAUCE, MUSHROOM STYLE

- 1 garlic clove, split
- 1 tablespoon olive oil
- 1 10-oz. can Italian sauce, mushroom style
- 1 8-oz. can tomato sauce
- 1 3-oz. can mushroom caps
- 2 teaspoons soy sauce
- a pinch of sugar
- salt and pepper
- ½ cup chicken broth, if desired

Simmer garlic in olive oil for 1 minute, using a saucepan. Discard garlic. Add all ingredients, mix well, and simmer 12 to 15 minutes over medium low heat, stirring occasionally. Taste and correct seasoning with salt and pepper before serving.

Note: For a richer sauce, add chicken broth.

Serves 4

ITALIAN SAUCE, MARINARA STYLE

20 min.

- 1 garlic clove, split
- 1 tablespoon olive oil
- 1 10-oz. can Italian sauce, marinara style
- 1 8-oz. can tomato sauce
- 1 chicken bouillon cube
- ¼ cup dry white wine
- a pinch of sugar
- a pinch of oregano
- salt and pepper

Simmer garlic in olive oil for 1 minute, using a saucepan. Discard garlic. Add all ingredients, mix well, and simmer 12 to 15 minutes over medium low heat, stirring occasionally. Taste and correct seasoning with salt and pepper before serving.

Serves 4

CURRY SAUCE

20 min.

- 1 cup chicken broth
- 2 tablespoons butter
- 2 tablespoons flour
- 1 teaspoon onion juice
- 3 tablespoons apple sauce
- bayleaf tip
- curry powder
- a slice of lime
- tiny pinch of cloves
- ½ teaspoon sugar
- salt and pepper

Start chicken broth heating. Melt butter in a second saucepan, add flour, blend smooth. Slowly add chicken broth, stirring constantly over medium heat until smooth. Add onion juice, apple sauce, and all other ingredients; use from 1 to 3 teaspoons curry powder, depending on your taste. Simmer 12 to 15 minutes over low heat, stirring occasionally. Taste and correct seasoning, adding salt and pepper and a little more sugar. Discard bayleaf and lime before serving. See below for serving suggestions.

Serves 3 or 4

CURRY SAUCE VARIATIONS

At the last moment before serving, add:

½ cup fruit cocktail well drained, or
8 or 10 stewed prunes, pitted and quartered, or
A handful of raisins, soaked in hot water for 5 minutes, or
½ cup chopped fresh pineapple, sweetened, or
1 or 2 fresh tomatoes, seeded, then chopped coarsely.

CURRY DINNER

To above Curry Sauce recipe add cooked diced lamb or fish, or canned chicken, shrimp, crab, or lobster meat. Heat thoroughly and serve over boiled rice, with chutney in a side dish. Add a green salad and a cake dessert to the meal.

Note: One to two cups of meat, fish, or fowl will serve 4.

10 min.

CANNED GRAVY

1 11-oz. can gravy
¼ teaspoon kitchen bouquet
½ teaspoon onion juice
salt and pepper
chicken broth, if desired

Combine all ingredients and simmer 7 or 8 minutes. Taste and correct seasoning with salt and pepper. Thin gravy with chicken broth, if desired.

Serves 4

GRAVY MADE WITH GRAVY POWDER

10 min.

Prepare gravy as directed on package, but use beef extract and water or chicken broth in place of half the water called for. Add ½ teaspoon onion juice for each cup.

1 cup serves 2 or 3

LIQUID "GRAVY MAKERS"

Hint

Prepare as directed on package, using pan drippings or meat juices if available. Otherwise, add liquid beef extract or bouillon cubes. Add ½ teaspoon onion juice for each cup of gravy. A chunk of butter makes a big difference in richness.

MUSHROOM GRAVY (Made with Canned Gravy)

15 min.

1 tablespoon butter
1 3-oz. can mushrooms
½ teaspoon onion juice
1 11-oz. can gravy
1 teaspoon soy sauce
salt and pepper

Melt butter in a saucepan, add mushrooms and liquid and all other ingredients. Simmer 10 to 12 minutes over low heat, stirring occasionally. Taste and correct seasoning with salt and pepper before serving.

Serves 4

ONION GRAVY (Made with Canned Gravy)

15 min.

2 medium-size onions, thinly sliced
2 tablespoons butter
1 11-oz. can gravy
1 teaspoon soy sauce
salt and pepper
sugar

Sauté onions in butter until nicely browned (about 6 minutes). Add gravy and soy sauce; simmer 5 minutes. Taste and correct seasoning with salt, pepper, and up to ½ teaspoon sugar. Simmer a minute or so after seasoning, and serve.

Serves 4 to 6

CANNED LIQUID GRAVY AS A BASE FOR MEAT DISHES

Time-saver

Where recipe calls for sauce to be made as part of the dish, omit sauce-making steps and use canned gravy instead. Season as directed in the recipe you're making, or prepare gravy as in Canned Gravy (see above).

Rice, Spaghetti and Macaroni

Packaged Pre-Cooked Rice

All groceries now sell packaged pre-cooked rice. There's nothing better to keep on your shelf, because this product not only *tastes* as rice should, but it needs no attention whatsoever while it "cooks"—and you can't go wrong. It comes out right every time!

Even quicker and easier to prepare is canned cooked rice. Look in the Oriental food section of your grocer's shelves; cooked rice is packed by the same people who put up Chow Mein and Chop Suey.

EXTRA RICH PACKAGED PRE-COOKED RICE

Hint

Use half chicken broth and half water for liquid, instead of plain water. Or, for creamed dishes with rice as an ingredient, add ½ cup milk to the water.

CANNED COOKED RICE—TO FRESHEN

6 min.

Put 2 cups water in a saucepan over highest heat to boil. Add ⅛ teaspoon salt. Add rice; when water boils, cook for 1 to 2 minutes, depending on whether you like firm or softer grains. Drain, and rice is ready to serve.

1 #2 can serves 4 to 6

One-dish Dinner

"RICE DINNER" (CANNED)

2 tablespoons butter
1 3-oz. can mushrooms, drained
¼ teaspoon onion juice
1 teaspoon soy sauce
1 16-oz. can "rice dinner"
1 cup or more cooked, chopped meat, chicken, fish, or cooked, shelled and deveined shrimp

12 min.

Melt butter in a saucepan, add mushrooms, onion juice, and soy sauce. Mix. Simmer 1 minute; add can of rice and meat, chicken, fish, or shrimp. Mix carefully; heat through over low heat and serve.

1 can serves 2

SPANISH RICE

1¾ cups tomato juice
2 fresh tomatoes
1 chicken bouillon cube
½ teaspoon salt; pepper
1 6-oz. package pre-cooked rice
1 tablespoon butter
1 green pepper, coarsely chopped
1 teaspoon onion juice
1 6-oz. can boned chicken

20 min.

Measure tomato juice into saucepan and place over highest heat. Cut tomatoes into coarse chunks and add to juice; add bouillon cube, salt, and a dusting of pepper. Pour rice into juice slowly, stirring constantly. Reduce heat slightly. When rice boils, cook 1 minute; remove from heat, cover pan tightly and let stand 10 minutes. Meanwhile melt butter in a large skillet, add green pepper and onion juice; cook over medium heat until pepper is soft (about 5 minutes). Add chicken, broken into coarse chunks. When rice is ready, turn into pepper-chicken mixture and mix well. Taste and correct seasoning with salt, heat through for a minute or so and serve.

Serves 6

SPANISH RICE WITH ANCHOVIES

18 min.

Prepare Spanish Rice (above). Omit chicken. Just before serving add 1 scant teaspoon capers and two 2-oz. cans anchovy filets drained of oil. If filets are rolled, cut across into quarters; if flat, cut into thirds. Toss mixture to combine and serve at once.

SHRIMP AND SPANISH RICE

20 min.

Prepare Spanish Rice (above). Omit chicken. When peppers are soft, add 1 or 2 cups cooked, shelled and deveined shrimp to skillet. Mix well and cook over low heat until rice mixture is ready.

CREAMED CHIPPED BEEF AND RICE

18 min.

2 cups water
1 #2 can cooked rice
1 recipe Creamed Chipped Beef (see Index)
bread crumbs and grated cheese, mixed
butter

Start broiler pre-heating to medium hot. Measure water into a saucepan and place over highest heat; when boiling add rice and freshen as directed on package. Prepare Creamed Chipped Beef. When ready, turn well-drained rice into a heatproof casserole, add meat mixture, combine; sprinkle top generously with bread crumb-grated cheese mixture and dot generously with butter. Place under broiler for 2 or 3 minutes, or until nicely browned.

Serves 4 to 6

18 min.

MUSHROOM AND RICE CASSEROLE

2 cups water
1 #2 can cooked rice
2 tablespoons butter
1 3-oz. can mushroom bits and pieces
1 3-oz. can mushroom caps
2 teaspoons soy sauce
1 can condensed mushroom soup
salt and pepper
bread crumbs and grated cheese, mixed

Start broiler pre-heating to medium hot. Measure water into saucepan and place over highest heat; when boiling add rice and freshen as directed on package. Meanwhile melt butter in another large saucepan, add mushrooms and soy sauce; combine and simmer 2 or 3 minutes. Add soup and rice, combine, taste and correct seasoning with salt and a dusting of pepper; heat thoroughly, stirring occasionally. To serve: turn into a heatproof casserole, sprinkle with bread crumb-grated cheese mixture and brown for a few moments under the broiler.

Serves 4 to 6

20 min.

LUXURY MUSHROOM CASSEROLE

Prepare Mushroom and Rice Casserole (above). To mushrooms and soy sauce mixture add, broken into chunks, one 6-oz. can boned chicken or one 8-oz. can tuna fish, well drained.

Serves 6

COOK RICE IN ADVANCE

Time-saver

Double the quantity of rice you need for a meal and store the leftover in the refrigerator, well covered with waxed paper. It will keep several days. When you want rice, reheat as directed in Canned Cooked Rice—To Freshen (see Index) omitting salt.

APPLE RICE

18 min.

(Serve as a garnish with broiled ham or pork chops)

- 1 cup canned "pie" apples
- ¾ cup water
- ¼ teaspoon salt
- ⅔ cup packaged pre-cooked rice
- a pinch of cinnamon
- 1 tablespoon butter
- sugar

Combine apples, water, and salt; bring to a boil over highest heat. Slowly stir in rice; simmer 1 minute, add cinnamon and butter; stir and remove from heat. Cover tightly and let stand 10 minutes. Just before serving, taste and correct seasoning (may need a little sugar if apples are very tart).

Serves 3 or 4

HAM AND APPLE RICE

18 min.

- 1 recipe Apple Rice (see above)
- ¾ pound or more thickly sliced boiled ham (or baked Virginia ham)
- butter
- salt

Prepare rice as directed. While rice is "cooking" off the heat, cut ham into 2 inch squares and turn into a hot skillet containing a generous lump of butter. Sprinkle a few grains of salt over ham to perk up the flavor. Brown meat slightly. To serve: make a mound of the rice on a serving platter, reserving a few spoonfuls; cover mound with ham and garnish with reserved rice.

Serves 3 or 4

SAUSAGES AND APPLE RICE

18 min.

- 1 recipe Apple Rice (see above)
- 2 8-oz. cans breakfast sausages

Prepare rice as directed. While rice is "cooking" off

the heat, brown sausages as directed on package, using broiler heat. To serve: make a rice ring (see Timesaver Index) and fill helter-skelter with sausages.

Serves 4

One-dish Dinner

RICE AND STEW POT

½ cup chicken broth
2 fresh tomatoes, chopped
1 #2 can beef or lamb stew
1 3-oz. can mushroom caps
1 cup cooked peas and carrots
⅔ cup packaged precooked rice
¾ cup water
¼ teaspoon salt
salt and pepper

20 min.

Put broth in a saucepan over highest heat to boil; add tomatoes, simmer 2 or 3 minutes. Add stew, mushrooms, peas and carrots; mix well; taste and correct seasoning with salt and pepper. Simmer until rice is ready. Meanwhile prepare rice as directed on package; using ¾ cup water and ¼ teaspoon salt. When rice is done, turn into stew; mix gently and serve.

Serves 4

15 min.

RICE RING WITH SAUCE

Cook one 6-oz. box packaged pre-cooked rice as directed on package. Meanwhile prepare Mushroom or Cottage Cheese Omelette Topping (see Index). When rice is ready, stir in 1 tablespoon butter and season lightly with salt and pepper. Make a Quick Rice Ring (see below) and turn omelette filling into center.

Serves 4

QUICK RICE RING

Time-saver

Place a bowl, the size of the ring you want to make, right side up on a platter. Spoon rice all around the base of the bowl, packing it in place *very* lightly. Gently twist bowl, then lift, and mold is ready. Easiest to do if the ring is made not more than 2 or 3 inches high.

RICE IN SOUP

Hint

Cooked leftover rice (or canned cooked rice refreshed as directed on the package) is an excellent extender for soup. If cooked rice is not available, just add packaged pre-cooked rice to boiling soups of the broth type. Simmer soup 5 to 7 minutes or until rice is tender.

Leftover Spanish rice or rice casseroles with a tomato-green pepper base find a very happy home in vegetable soups or chowders.

Spaghetti

PACKAGED READY-PREPARED SPAGHETTI DINNER

20 min.

To cook the spaghetti: Add half a small clove of garlic to the water, which should be generously salted.

To season the sauce: Add to the sauce in the package:

1 small can mushrooms and liquid
2 teaspoons butter
¼ teaspoon salt
a pinch of oregano
½ teaspoon sugar
if sauce is thick add ½ cup plain chicken broth or tomato sauce

Combine all ingredients and simmer 10 minutes.

To season the cheese: A pinch of salt mixed through the cheese helps bring out the flavor.

Note: For spaghetti dinner at home with no cooking involved except for the spaghetti, go to your favorite Italian restaurant and buy sauce to take out, allowing about 1 pint for each 4 persons. This sauce keeps well, and may be purchased a day or so in advance of using, if stored in the coldest part of the refrigerator.

1 package serves 3 or 4

Hints

WATCH SPAGHETTI COOKING TIME

Don't overcook spaghetti so that it becomes mushy. Accurately follow cooking time on package, or, if you can buy that wonderful long-strand "bulk" spaghetti from an Italian grocery, follow these times:

Regular spaghetti: Cook from 12 to 18 minutes

Spaghettini (thin spaghetti): Cook from 8 to 13 minutes.

Bite a strand to test the done-ness. When it's tender but not mushy, it is sufficiently cooked. Remove from heat at once and drain. Rinsing is not needed if cooked in plenty of water.

When cooking spaghetti, don't break it into short pieces, because it is actually easier to eat when served in long strands. To fit the strands into a "too-small" pan, place ends in boiling water and push gently. As the water softens the spaghetti, it will curl right around the inside of the pan.

SPAGHETTI WITH ANCHOVIES

1 8-oz. package "thin" spaghetti
1 recipe Italian Sauce, Mushroom or Marinara Style (see Index)
1 or 2 2-oz. cans anchovy filets

Put water on to boil for spaghetti; cook as directed on package. Meanwhile prepare sauce. When ready, drain anchovy filets of oil and cut into thirds. Add to sauce, stir lightly, and pour over drained spaghetti. Serve at once. For a garnish, reserve a few bits of anchovy.

20 min.

Serves 4

FOR QUICK COOKING USE SPAGHETTINI

Hint

Spaghettini *is* spaghetti, except that it is much thinner, hence cooks in less time. Popular brands of spaghettini are usually described as "thin" on the label.

Many cooks prefer spaghettini not only for the cooking time it saves, but for the professional "finish" it adds to a spaghetti dish.

SPAGHETTI WITH CHICKEN LIVERS

1 8-oz. package "thin" spaghetti
1 recipe Italian Sauce, Mushroom or Marinara Style (see Index)
2 tablespoons butter
1 package (½ pound) frozen chicken livers, thawed

Put water on to boil for spaghetti; cook as directed on package. Meanwhile prepare sauce. While sauce is simmering, sauté livers in butter over low heat. Cut livers in halves or quarters, if preferred. Turn livers once while cooking for 5 to 8 minutes, or until just done. Do not overcook. Turn sauce into skillet con-

20 min.

taining livers and mix gently. Simmer 2 or 3 minutes and serve poured over spaghetti.

Note: As few as 3 or 4 livers (cut into large dice) may be used, if wanted only for an added touch to the sauce.

Serves 4 to 6

10 min.

CANNED SPAGHETTI

¼ cup chicken broth
¼ cup water
1 3-oz. can mushrooms, drained
½ teaspoon soy sauce
pinch of celery salt
1 tablespoon butter
1 #2 can spaghetti
salt and pepper
grated cheese

Combine broth, water, mushrooms, soy sauce, and celery salt in a saucepan. Simmer over low heat for 2 minutes. Add butter and spaghetti; mix gently and heat thoroughly. Taste and correct seasoning with salt and a light dusting of pepper. Serve with grated cheese on the side.

1 #2 can serves 2 or 3

Macaroni

15 min.

PACKAGED MACARONI DINNER

Put water for macaroni on to boil. Start broiler pre-heating to medium hot.

To prepare the macaroni: Boil as directed on package, adding a small onion to the water. Drain, discarding onion. Add:

1 tablespoon butter
¼ cup light cream or sour cream
1 teaspoon chopped parsley
salt and pepper

Mix macaroni with all ingredients, seasoning lightly with salt and pepper.

To season the cheese: Taste cheese. If salt is needed, add up to 1/4 teaspoon. If cheese seems to be too sharp for your taste, dilute it with very fine bread crumbs.

To serve: Reserve 2 tablespoons cheese. Combine remainder of cheese with macaroni mixture and turn into a heatproof casserole. Mix 1 tablespoon bread crumbs with reserved cheese, sprinkle over macaroni, dot generously with butter, and brown under the broiler.

1 package serves 3 or 4

CANNED MACARONI AND CHEESE

Hint

If this product is available in your grocery, sharpen the flavor by turning into a casserole, heating in a moderate oven, and spreading liberally with grated or diced sharp Cheddar. Place under medium broiler heat for a few minutes, or until cheese bubbles slightly.

TOMATO MACARONI

15 min.

1 package macaroni dinner
1 3-oz. can mushrooms
1 3-oz. can tomato sauce
1 #2 can whole pack tomatoes
butter
salt and pepper

Put water for macaroni on to boil over highest heat. In a saucepan combine mushrooms, tomato sauce, and tomatoes, quartered. Place over medium heat. When it boils, add about 1/2 cup macaroni and simmer 10 minutes or until macaroni is tender. Cook remainder of macaroni in boiling water, adding a small onion. When the macaroni is ready, drain, discard onion, add a generous chunk of butter, a light dusting of salt and pepper. Mix; add tomato-macaroni mixture; mix again. Serve with cheese on the side, seasoned as directed in Packaged Macaroni Dinner (above). Or, sprinkle top with a few teaspoons of cheese mixed with a little bread crumbs and brown under the broiler for a few minutes.

Serves 3 or 4

CHEESE SAUCE FOR MACARONI

Hint

See Index for a rich Cheese Sauce to serve over macaroni. If using a macaroni dinner, save the grated cheese that comes in the package for another dish, or use it as part of the cheese sauce. To serve: combine the macaroni with about ¾ of the sauce; pour the remainder over the top.

"GRATING" CHEESE

Hint

If you can find genuine Parmesan or Romano cheese, buy a one-pound chunk or so, and grate cheese as you need it. Wrap it well in foil, and the cheese will keep for months in the refrigerator.

CANNED RAVIOLI

12 min.

Prepare sauce for Canned Spaghetti (see Index). When ready, add one 16-oz. jar ravioli. Simmer two minutes; dip out ravioli and set aside while combining *your* sauce and ravioli sauce thoroughly. Return ravioli to pan; heat thoroughly, and serve.

1 jar serves 2 or 3

Griddle Cakes

Hints

UTENSILS

Use a griddle. Not a skillet, if at all possible. Griddles are designed for this kind of cookery; most important of all, you can make bigger batches and save time!

The most practical griddle is made of magnesium metal, in a rectangular shape large enough to span two burners on most stoves. When used this way, food on the center of a magnesium griddle cooks as quickly and evenly as the food on the parts of the griddle directly over the burners. That's because magnesium is a very efficient conductor of heat.

TEMPERATURE OF THE GRIDDLE

Unless you are a skilled judge of griddle temperature, bake a small test cake first to see if the griddle is hot enough. If the cake bakes with the brown and white "spider-web" pattern you've seen so often in pictures of griddle cakes, the temperature is right. *Don't guess! No* griddle cake has ever survived being baked with too much or too little heat.

BUTTER OR SHORTENING

Cook with butter, or if you object to some smoke, use vegetable shortening. Griddle or skillet should be greased lightly between each batch. An easy way to do it is to crumple a small clean brown paper bag into a pad, dab on some butter or shortening, and use the bag as a swab. Discard bag when through.

WHEN TO TURN GRIDDLE CAKES

Don't bake cakes until they're dried out on top. When the tops are still moist, but bubbly, turn the cakes. Use a wide spatula to handle cakes—and turn them only once. The second side requires about half the time of the first, since, when the top bubbles, the cake is just about cooked through.

HOW TO SERVE GRIDDLE CAKES

Be generous with the butter and syrup. Heat syrup slightly for a better flavor. See below for a hint about Thrifty Butter Service.

Above all, have cakes piping hot. Serve at once; don't let baked cakes stand. And it's better to serve a man-size stack to *one* person at a time, than merely to tease everybody's appetite by dividing up a batch of griddle cakes.

HOW TO TOSS GRIDDLE CAKES

It's easier than you think. The secret is to loosen the cake with a spatula, then toss with just enough "lift" to raise the cake above the pan. It will turn over automatically. Just be sure to have the *pan* under the cake when it comes down.

PANCAKES *(Biscuit Mix)*

- 1 egg
- 1¾ cups milk
- ½ teaspoon sugar
- ⅛ teaspoon salt
- 2 cups biscuit mix
- 1 or 2 tablespoons melted butter

Beat egg, milk, sugar, and salt together; add to mix and beat lightly (lumps come out in the baking). Stir in butter. Bake on a hot lightly buttered griddle until bubbly but moist on top; turn once and bake a few minutes longer.

12 min.

Makes 12 to 16

TO ADD MELTED BUTTER TO GRIDDLE CAKE MIXES

If baking cakes in a skillet, melt butter in skillet and pour into mix; if baking cakes on a griddle, measure butter into a tea or custard cup, place in a saucepan containing about ½ inch water and place pan over highest heat. Do this before you start mixing the batter; by the time you're ready for the butter it will be melted.

Time-saver

PANCAKES *(Pancake Mix)*

- 1 egg
- milk for liquid (see package for amount)
- ½ teaspoon sugar
- ⅛ teaspoon salt
- 2 cups pancake mix
- 1 or 2 tablespoons melted butter

Beat egg, milk, sugar, and salt together; add to mix and beat lightly (lumps come out in the baking). Stir in butter. Bake on a hot lightly buttered griddle until cakes are bubbly but moist on top; turn once and bake a few minutes longer.

12 min.

Makes 12 to 16

THRIFTY PANCAKE SYRUP

1 pound light brown sugar (or dark brown sugar for a more robust flavor)	1 cup water
	½ teaspoon salt
	2 teaspoons maple flavoring

10 min.

Stir all ingredients together; bring to a simmer and cook gently for 6 minutes. Remove from heat, skim, and serve in a pitcher.

Note: Bottle and seal leftover syrup. It keeps well without refrigeration for 2 or 3 weeks.

Makes 1 pint

THRIFTY BUTTER SERVICE

Hint

Serve butter this way and actually use less without stinting anyone: allow one generous pat of butter for each person; melt the butter in a serving bowl placed in a pan of boiling water. Serve with a small pastry brush in the bowl, for brushing butter onto the cakes.

Or, if your family insists on *seeing* the butter melt on the pancakes, mash together equal parts of softened yellow margarine and butter; form into pats and drop into cold water before serving.

CORNMEAL PANCAKES I

1 package corn muffin mix	⅛ teaspoon salt
1 egg	1 tablespoon melted butter
milk	

12 min.

Use amount of milk called for on package in pancake recipe, or, for a 12-oz. package of mix, use about ¾ cup milk. Beat egg, milk, and salt together, add to mix and beat lightly (lumps come out in the baking). Stir in butter. Bake on a hot lightly buttered griddle until bubbly but moist on top; turn once and bake a few minutes longer.

Note: Cornmeal griddle cakes are richer and more filling; make cakes slightly smaller.

Makes 12 to 16

PANCAKE "CHANGE-OFF"

Hint

Add 4 strips of crisp bacon, crumbled, to pancake batter, just before baking.

Add ½ cup well-drained berries or fruit to batter.

Add thinly sliced well-browned canned breakfast sausages to batter.

Add ½ cup chopped apple to batter.

COOKED-CEREAL "PANCAKES"

Time-saver

When preparing breakfast cereal, double the recipe; pour the extra into a loaf shaped container and store in refrigerator. To make "pancakes," slice chilled cereal and fry in plenty of butter until nicely browned; 1 cup of cooked cereal will make 6 to 8 slices.

Eggs

When you're short of cooking time, a repertoire of tasty, exciting-looking egg dishes is a 20-minute cook's best friend.

With eggs serve a green vegetable, Four-Minute Fried Potatoes (see Index)—add a whipped cream dessert, and you'll please even a "meat n' potatoes" man (most of the time).

MONEY-SAVING EGG TRICKS

Hint

When you buy eggs, ask for the "medium" size. There is usually several cents difference in the price, and you get practically as much egg for your money.

If you live in an area where consumers insist on eggs of a certain color and pay a premium for them (in Boston, for example, *brown* eggs are considered choice), *you* buy eggs opposite in color to those in demand. They'll sell for less. Dietetically or any other way, there is no difference between brown and white eggs except in the color of the shell.

SEASONINGS FOR SCRAMBLED EGGS

Hints

When adding cream, use sour instead of sweet cream for richer flavor.

Add 1/4 teaspoon curry powder or 1/4 teaspoon prepared mustard to each 6 eggs when beating for scrambling.

Replace 1/4 teaspoon salt in egg recipe with 1/2 teaspoon celery salt.

When poaching eggs, use milk, tomato juice, or thinned canned soup instead of water. Save the liquid for a sauce base.

Add 1 teaspoon mayonnaise to each 4 eggs when beating for scrambling.

Use freshly ground pepper for best flavor.

Add 2 tablespoons canned mushroom liquid to each 4 eggs when beating for scrambling.

Add 1 teaspoon or slightly more finely chopped chives or watercress when beating eggs for scrambling; or add dehydrated parsley.

SCRAMBLED EGGS

2 tablespoons butter
6 or 8 eggs
2 tablespoons sweet or sour cream
½ teaspoon salt
¼ teaspoon pepper

10 min.

Melt butter in a large skillet over medium heat. Meanwhile beat all ingredients together until well blended. (Use sour cream if possible.) When butter just begins to brown, add eggs; cook, stirring constantly with a spoon, turning bottom to top. When eggs are moist but firm, they are ready. Don't overcook. Turn eggs onto warmed plate at once (they will continue to cook if left in a hot skillet).

Serves 4

SCRAMBLED EGGS WITH ONION FLAVOR—VARIATION

To butter in skillet add 2 or 3 thin slices of onion and simmer gently while preparing scrambled egg mixture. Cook onion until soft and scramble eggs with it, or discard before turning eggs into skillet.

SCRAMBLED EGGS IN BLACK BUTTER

6 or 8 eggs	½ teaspoon salt
2 tablespoons butter	¼ teaspoon pepper

Note: Have everything ready, including warmed serving plates, before starting this recipe.

Place a large skillet, without butter, over high heat to pre-heat. Break eggs into a bowl; puncture yolks with a fork but do not beat. Turn butter into skillet and let it brown until almost black. Sprinkle salt and pepper into skillet. Pour in eggs all at once; quickly scramble together, using a fork, and mixing yolks with whites. Cooking occurs very quickly, so watch carefully. When moist but firm, eggs are ready. Turn out of skillet at once.

10 min.

Serves 4

KEEP EGGS COLD

Always keep eggs covered, in the coldest part of the refrigerator. Buy them in a store where they're kept under refrigeration. Don't wipe eggs before storing—you'll remove a natural coating over the shell pores which helps preserve them.

Hint

ANCHOVY SCRAMBLED EGGS

6 or 8 eggs	¼ teaspoon pepper
2 tablespoons sour cream	2 tablespoons butter
1 teaspoon anchovy paste or less	rolled anchovy filets, if desired
⅛ teaspoon salt	

Melt butter in a large skillet over medium heat. Beat all ingredients, first stirring sour cream and anchovy paste together. When butter browns slightly, add eggs; cook, stirring constantly with a spoon, turning bottom to top. When eggs are moist but firm, they

20 min.

are ready. Don't overcook. Turn eggs onto a warmed plate at once and garnish with anchovy filets, well drained, if desired.

Serves 4 to 6

15 min.

SCRAMBLED EGGS WITH SPINACH

1 tablespoon butter
¾ cup more or less well-drained cooked frozen spinach, leaf variety preferred
6 eggs
2 tablespoons sweet or sour cream
½ teaspoon salt
pepper
1 tablespoon butter

Melt butter in skillet, add spinach (if not previously seasoned, dust lightly with salt and pepper). Cook over medium heat 5 minutes, stirring frequently. Meanwhile beat eggs, cream, salt, and a light dusting of pepper together. Add second tablespoon of butter to skillet; when melted, add eggs and scramble until firm but not dry. Serve at once.

Serves 4 to 6

15 min.

SCRAMBLED EGGS WITH TOMATOES

1 #2 can whole-pack tomatoes
3 tablespoons butter
¼ teaspoon onion juice
½ teaspoon salt
¼ teaspoon pepper
a pinch of nutmeg
6 eggs

Drain tomatoes well, saving the liquid for another dish. Cut into large chunks, simmer 5 minutes in a saucepan to which has been added half the butter, onion juice, and seasonings. Beat eggs lightly; scramble in a hot skillet with remainder of butter. When eggs start to solidify, pour in the tomatoes; scramble all together, gently stirring until eggs are firm and moist.

Serves 4

HONEY BISCUITS WITH EGGS

Hint

This combination is "dressy" enough for guests—and there's no better (or quicker) TV snack. See Index for Honey Biscuit recipe (quicker if you make dropped biscuits). Use Scrambled Eggs or Scrambled Eggs in Black Butter (see above).

CREAM CHEESE EGGS

15 min.

- 3-oz. package cream cheese
- 3 tablespoons milk
- 6 eggs
- ½ teaspoon salt
- ¼ teaspoon pepper
- 2 tablespoons butter
- 1 teaspoon chopped parsley

In mixing bowl, soften cheese with milk. Add 2 eggs, and using a rotary beater, beat eggs, cheese, and milk together until smooth. Add remainder of eggs and seasonings; beat again until well combined. Scramble in butter in a hot skillet; when firm but not quite dry enough to serve, add parsley and combine; continue cooking until ready.

Serves 4

OMELET FOR TOPPING

(See Topping Recipes Below)

20 min.

- 6 egg whites
- 6 egg yolks
- ½ teaspoon salt
- ¼ teaspoon pepper
- ¼ cup water
- 1 generous tablespoon butter
- paprika

Start oven pre-heating to medium. Beat whites until stiff enough to hold a soft peak. Beat yolks until lemon-colored, add salt, pepper, and water. Fold yolks into whites. Meanwhile melt butter in skillet over low heat. Turn egg mixture gently into skillet, raise heat to medium and cook 3 minutes. Place skillet in oven for 7 to 10 minutes, or until top of omelet is firm and dry to the touch. To serve: loosen edges of omelet and slip onto warmed platter. Cut into pie-shaped wedges, one for each serving. Sprinkle with a little paprika. At the table, serve each person a wedge and spoon on the topping which you have meanwhile prepared.

Serves 4 to 6

14 min.

MUSHROOM OMELET-TOPPING

2 tablespoons butter
3 thin slices onion
½ teaspoon soy sauce
1 3-oz. can mushroom pieces
1 3-oz. can mushroom caps
1 teaspoon flour

Melt butter in a saucepan, add onion and simmer 3 or 4 minutes, or until onion softens. Drain liquid from mushrooms into a bowl; add mushrooms to onions. Into mushroom liquid stir flour, and add to mixture in saucepan. Stir until smooth. Simmer 8 to 10 minutes over low heat, stirring occasionally. Taste and correct seasoning—serve piping hot.

Serves 4 to 6

12 min.

COTTAGE CHEESE OMELET-TOPPING

1 tablespoon butter
3 thin slices onion
2 tablespoons chopped green pepper
¼ cup heavy sweet cream
½ teaspoon salt
pepper
uncreamed (popcorn style) cottage cheese

Melt butter in a saucepan, add onion and green pepper and simmer 5 minutes or until soft. Add cream, salt, and a generous dusting of pepper; mix. Stir in cottage cheese. Heat through, stirring gently. Keep hot over low heat until omelet is ready.

Serves 4 to 6

SMOKED SALMON (LOX) OMELET-TOPPING

4 to 6 thin slices (about ¼ lb.) smoked salmon	2 tablespoons butter
milk, if needed	2 thin slices onion
	3 tablespoons heavy cream

Trim bones and fat from salmon. If fish is the saltier domestic variety, soak in a little milk for 3 or 4 minutes; discard milk. Meanwhile melt butter in a saucepan, add onion, and cook 3 or 4 minutes or until soft. Add fish, and cook until it turns light pink, stirring with a fork to break flesh into bits. Remove from heat until omelet is ready. Just before serving, add heavy cream and stir lightly. Heat through and serve.

15 min.

Note: Sour cream may be used instead of sweet; do not boil sauce after adding.

Serves 4 to 6

OMELET-TOPPINGS—VARIATIONS

(See Omelet for Topping, Above)

SPANISH: Prepare Quick Creole Sauce (see Index), reserving about ½ cup for another dish. Top omelet with remainder, piping hot.

VEGETABLE: Use any cooked vegetable, heated in a little cream and seasoned rather highly with salt and pepper. Allow about ⅓ cup per portion. Best varieties are peas, lima beans, snap beans, or spinach.

CHEESE: Spoon Cheese Sauce (see Index) over each portion; 1 cup of sauce serves 4.

HAM: Heat thinly sliced boiled ham, coarsely chopped, in a little butter. Sprinkle very lightly with salt and top each omelet portion with about ¼ cup.

BACON: Heat bacon-rind cocktail snacks in the oven

for a few minutes; sprinkle very lightly with salt and top each portion with about 1/4 cup.

CORN: Do as for bacon, with crisp corn cocktail snacks.

ONION: If you have the extra time, prepare frozen French-fried onion rings as directed on the package; sprinkle the crisp rings over the omelet.

Timesaver: Heat canned French-fried cocktail onion snacks and sprinkle over the omelet.

Salads

Salad is the magic course that makes it possible for a seemingly "light" meal to satisfy hungry people. A tossed salad should look like just that—but take a little care in the preparation. Have salad greens crisp and as chilled as possible; cut vegetables evenly; serve the salad heaped up in large bowls and be sure there's plenty of salad dressing.

Bottled salad dressings vary in taste from brand to brand. So, when you find a flavor you like, stick to it. Don't guess when adjusting flavors. Salad dressing is either right or not (you can't "take back" too much seasoning).

Ready-Prepared Salad Dressings

HOW TO ADJUST THE FLAVOR OF OIL-TYPE DRESSINGS

Hint

If dressing seems *too bland* add one of the following to each 3 tablespoons:

a pinch of salt
a pinch of dry mustard
leave a bit of crushed garlic clove in dressing 2 or 3 minutes, then discard
a pea-size bit of anchovy paste
⅛ teaspoon or less onion juice
⅛ teaspoon curry powder
herbs as in Optional Ingredients for French Dressing (see below)

If dressing seems *too tart* add to each 3 tablespoons:

1 to 2 teaspoons olive or safflower oil

If dressing is *not tart enough* add one of the following to each 3 tablespoons:

1 teaspoon wine vinegar
½ teaspoon lemon juice

(*Note:* Vinegar or lemon juice varies in potency; add a little at a time and taste as you go.)

If dressing is *not rich enough* add one of the following to each 3 tablespoons:

1 to 2 teaspoons sour cream
1 to 2 teaspoons mayonnaise

Method: Measure dressing into a shallow dish. Add seasoning ingredient and whisk well with a fork to mix. Taste. Correct seasoning, if necessary.

HOW TO ADJUST THE FLAVOR OF CREAM-TYPE DRESSINGS

If dressing seems *too bland* add one of the following to each ¼ cup:

a few grains of salt
a tiny pinch of dry mustard dissolved in ½ teaspoon cream
⅛ teaspoon or less onion juice
⅛ teaspoon or slightly more curry powder
herbs, finely ground, as in optional ingredients for French Dressing (see below)

If dressing seems *too tart* add to each ¼ cup:

1 to 2 teaspoons sweet heavy cream

If dressing is *not tart enough* add one of the following to each ¼ cup:

½ teaspoon wine vinegar
¼ to ½ teaspoon lemon juice

(Note: Vinegar or lemon juice varies in potency; add a little at a time and taste as you go.)

If dressing is *not rich enough* add one of the following to each 1/4 cup:

- 1 to 2 teaspoons sweet cream
- 1 to 2 teaspoons mayonnaise

Method: Measure dressing into shallow dish. Add seasoning ingredient and whisk thoroughly with a fork to mix. Taste. Correct seasoning if necessary.

Timesaver: When you have finally adjusted the flavor of prepared salad dressing to suit, make a note of what you added, in the proportions for the quantity of dressing you usually prepare. Paste this information on the inside of your kitchen cupboard, and you'll save having to check your cook book each time.

SALAD OILS

The *real* base of salad dressing is oil; hence, *what* oil you use affects the goodness of the finished salad. The basic requirement is that whatever oil you use be of impeccable freshness and fine quality.

If olive oil, splurge on virgin olive oil (it comes from the first pressing of the olives). It is costly, but worth it, since a little goes a long way. By the way, don't be fooled by the word "pure" or "imported" on the label. Only virgin olive oil is marked "virgin."

Hint

Peanut oil, or olive and peanut oils mixed also make a superior dressing.

Safflower oil makes an elegant salad dressing. Health considerations aside, safflower oil's faint hint of nut-sweet flavor and exceptional lightness combine to make a salad dressing worthy of the finest classic cuisine.

FRENCH DRESSINGS FOR SALADS

(*Your own "Ready-Prepared" Salad Dressing*)

8 min.

THESE INGREDIENTS ARE BASIC—USE THEM ALL

To make	½ cup	½ pint	1 pint
olive, peanut or safflower oil	6 tablespoons	¾ cup	1½ cups
wine vinegar	2 tablespoons	¼ cup	½ cup
garlic	half a small clove, crushed	1 small clove, crushed	2 small cloves, crushed
dry mustard	⅛ teaspoon	¼ teaspoon	½ teaspoon
chopped parsley	pinch	¼ teaspoon	½ teaspoon
salt	½ teaspoon	1 teaspoon	2 teaspoons
pepper	pinch	¼ teaspoon, scant	½ teaspoon, scant
sugar	pinch	¼ teaspoon, scant	½ teaspoon, scant

THESE INGREDIENTS ARE OPTIONAL, FOR VARIATIONS

onion juice	⅛ teaspoon	¼ teaspoon	½ teaspoon
chervil, tarragon, curry powder, dill	a pinch of one	¼ teaspoon of one	½ teaspoon of one
anchovy paste	¼ teaspoon, scant	½ teaspoon, scant	⅞ teaspoon
roquefort cheese, crumbled	1 tablespoon	2 tablespoons	¼ cup

Put all ingredients into a clean glass jar. Screw cap on tightly, shake very well. Discard garlic and serve or store. For more garlic flavor, let clove remain in the dressing for a while.

This dressing keeps well in the refrigerator. Shake well before using. If oil solidifies because of the cold, let dressing stand at room temperature until liquid again.

¼ cup dresses salad for 2 or 3

HOW TO MAKE YOUR OWN WINE VINEGAR

Hint

If you can't get wine vinegar in your locality, buy a fifth or a jug of dry sauterne, burgundy, or claret, any good domestic brand. Open bottle, add 3 tablespoons cider vinegar, cover top of bottle with gauze (do not seal) and allow to stand undisturbed for a dozen weeks or so in a cool dark place. You'll have fine, fragrant, mild wine vinegar. Some prefer to add a few peppercorns and a clove or two to the wine when adding cider vinegar.

HOW MUCH SALAD DRESSING SHOULD YOU USE?

Hint

All the salad ingredients should be barely "coated" with dressing. Judge it with your eye—greens will have a glossy appearance when salad is right. If salad seems dry, add a little more dressing and toss again.

If you prefer a rule, a safe one is ¼ cup dressing for 2 or 3 people. Use a little more for porous foods, such as fish or potatoes; a little less for greens.

Note: If salad stands in the refrigerator for a few minutes before serving, always toss it again, since dressing tends to drain to bottom of salad bowl. Don't let salad greens stand when coated with dressing. For best results, add dressing and toss salad at the table. (It's a good way to show off, too!)

SALAD INGREDIENTS GUIDE

12 min.

Use any of the following alone, or in combination.

For added flavor, marinate salad ingredients (except greens) in dressing if time permits. Greens become limp when coated with dressing, so combine greens with other salad ingredients at the last minute before serving.

Have salad ingredients chilled for the best taste.

GREENS:

Head or leaf lettuce, shredded or torn into bits.
Chicory, one part to three of lettuce.
Romaine, instead of lettuce.
Finely shredded tender young green or red cabbage, or coarsely chopped watercress; a few tablespoons of each.
Coarsely chopped celery leaves from the hearts.

RAW VEGETABLES:

Sliced radishes.
Chopped or razor-thin slices of Texas, Bermuda, or green onions.
Chopped celery.
Uncooked frozen peas, thawed.
Tomatoes, seeded and sliced or chopped.
Cucumbers, sliced or chopped.
Young and tender raw carrots, scraped, shaved, or thinly sliced.

COOKED VEGETABLES:

Lima beans, cooked, or canned green limas, drained and rinsed.
"Frenched" snap beans, frozen, cooked.
Canned snap beans, drained and rinsed.
Canned drained diced, sliced, or chopped beets.
Pickled Beets (see Index).
Frozen Peas, cooked, or canned peas, drained and rinsed.
Canned Chinese bean sprouts, well drained.

OTHER INGREDIENTS:

Chopped chilled leftover or canned meat, fish, or fowl.
Diced, julienned, or shredded cheese.
Cooked rice.
Cooked macaroni.

GARNISHES:

Green or ripe olives, pitted, chopped, if desired.
Pimiento strips.
Green pepper rings.
Onion rings.
Fresh parsley.
Celery leaves from the hearts.
Toasted bread cubes or croutons (see Index).
Cubes of the meat, fish, or fowl used.

Note: For best results, let your salad contain a little of several ingredients, although there's no rule about it. Let your own taste (and your supply of leftovers) be your guide.

2 or 3 cups serve 3 or 4

HOW TO MAKE "FANCY" CUCUMBERS

Hint

Wash an unpeeled cucumber well; using a fork with sharp tines, score the cucumber along its length, all the way around. The deeper the scores, the deeper the "scalloping." Slice thinly, without peeling.

TO CHILL SALAD INGREDIENTS QUICKLY

Time-saver

Pack into ice cube trays and place in freezing compartment; stir every few minutes, turning bottom to top. Do not allow to freeze.

TO KEEP GREENS FRESH

Hint

If your refrigerator hasn't a crisping bin, rinse greens in cold water, place in a brown paper bag, soak outside of bag with water. Wrap snugly with waxed paper, store in refrigerator. Greens will keep perfectly for several days.

GARLIC FOR OIL-TYPE DRESSINGS

Time-saver

Prepare "garlic oil" by placing 2 quartered cloves of garlic in ½ cup olive or peanut oil. Allow to stand in a warm place for a week; remove garlic, and use oil as a flavoring agent in salad dressings. A teaspoon or so will do the trick.

GARLIC FOR CREAM-TYPE DRESSINGS

Hint

Cut several gashes in a medium-size clove of garlic. Thrust into a fresh half-pint jar of mayonnaise (not salad dressing) and store in refrigerator for a week. Discard garlic, mix mayonnaise well, and use as a seasoning agent in cream-type dressings.

Impale the garlic clove on a toothpick and you can find it easily. *And label the jar!*

5 min.

QUICK SALAD

- 2 to 3 cups salad greens, any variety
- 3 tablespoons olive or peanut oil
- 1 tablespoon wine vinegar
- salt and pepper

Shred greens coarsely. Sprinkle with oil. Toss, then sprinkle with vinegar and a light dusting of salt and pepper. Toss again. Serve at once.

Serves 4

15 min.

CHEF'S SALAD

This salad is so named, likely, because a chef hit on this way to use up a batch of leftovers. Practically anything edible can be used in addition to the items listed in Salad Ingredients (see above). For best results, use a combination of greens, meat or fish, cheese, and vegetables (4 cups serve 3 or 4). Mix in a big bowl with plenty of dressing, and make plenty!

4 cups serve 3 or 4

COLE SLAW

15 min.

- ½ small head young red or white cabbage, or some of both
- ½ cup sweet or sour cream
- ½ teaspoon celery seeds
- 3 tablespoons French Dressing (see Index)
- 1 teaspoon onion juice
- 1 tablespoon chopped green pepper
- salt and pepper

The finer you shred the cabbage (after cutting away the core), the better. Mix all other ingredients well, add cabbage, toss. Chill slightly, if desired, in an ice cube tray. Toss again before serving.

Serves 6

EGG SALAD

12 min.

- 6 hard-cooked eggs, chilled
- 1 tablespoon mayonnaise
- 2 tablespoons heavy cream
- 1 tablespoon sour cream
- 1 teaspoon onion juice
- ¼ teaspoon celery seeds
- ¼ cup chopped celery
- salt and pepper

Quarter eggs, remove yolks; chop whites fine and return to refrigerator. Mash yolks, add all ingredients; mix, taste, and correct seasoning. Add whites; mix and serve on lettuce leaves or stuffed into tomatoes. Or use as sandwich filling.

Serves 4

TO CHILL HARD COOKED EGGS QUICKLY

Time-saver

Quarter eggs; remove yolks; drop whites into cold or ice water, or chop whites and place in ice cube tray for a few minutes. Mash yolks and spread out—they will cool to room temperature quickly.

15 to 20 min.

JELLIED EGG SALAD

2 cans consommé Madrilene, well chilled

1 recipe Egg Salad (see above)

If consommé is not chilled, turn into an ice cube tray and place in freezing compartment of refrigerator. Stir occasionally. It should be firm enough to serve in 15 to 18 minutes. Meanwhile prepare egg salad. To serve: spoon large "chunks" of the jellied consommé into a serving dish; top with spoonfuls of egg salad.

Serves 6

STUFFED EGGS

1 recipe Egg Salad (see above), adding 2 more eggs, if desired

½ teaspoon anchovy paste
anchovy filets

12 min.

Cut eggs in half the long way. Remove yolks and return whites to the refrigerator. Prepare yolk mixture as directed, adding anchovy paste. Stuff whites when ready to serve and garnish with bits of anchovy filet, well drained.

Serves 4

STUFFED EGGS FOR BACKYARD DINING (OR PICNICS)

Hint

Prepare Stuffed Eggs (see above). Serve with yolk filling in a bowl (fluff the top with a fork); surround the bowl with egg whites sprinkled with a bit of paprika. Fill the eggs yourself or let everybody help himself.

KEEP HARD COOKED EGGS ON HAND

When making boiled eggs for the family breakfast, add some extra eggs to the water. Let these cook hard; store in refrigerator and they'll be ready-chilled when you want them.

Time-saver

POTATO SALAD

1 #2 can boiled baby potatoes
¼ cup mayonnaise
¼ cup sour cream
¼ to ½ cup chopped celery
2 teaspoons onion juice
1 teaspoon celery salt
¼ teaspoon celery seed
salt and pepper
chopped parsley

Drain potatoes, rinse in cold water, and dice. If not chilled, turn into an ice cube tray and place in freezing compartment for 5 minutes. Meanwhile combine all other ingredients, mixing well. Add potatoes, toss lightly to avoid crushing, and keep salad in refrigerator until ready to serve.

15 min.

Note: The dressing in this salad makes an excellent change-off for a green salad. Dressing may be made in advance and stored in refrigerator for a few days.

Serves 4 to 6

SOUR CREAM SPRING SALAD

½ cup radishes, sliced
1 medium cucumber, sliced
1 bunch scallions, sliced thin
1 small head lettuce, shredded
1 pint sour cream
½ teaspoon salt; pepper
⅛ teaspoon celery seed

15 min.

Combine all the vegetables. To sour cream add 1 teaspoon salt, a generous shake of pepper, and celery seeds. Add to vegetables, toss to combine, and serve. Very refreshing in summer!

Serves 4

15 min.

TOMATOES STUFFED WITH SARDINES

4 large tomatoes, chilled
2 or 3 cans extra-quality oil-pack sardines
1 teaspoon lemon juice
½ cup seasoned cottage cheese or leftover egg salad
black olives

Slice tops off tomatoes, remove insides, and seed. Drain sardine oil into a bowl, add lemon juice and whisk to mix. Mix cottage cheese or egg salad with tomato insides and spoon a little into each tomato. Dip sardines in oil-lemon mixture and stand tails up in each tomato. Tuck a few spoonfuls of cheese or egg salad into centers and garnish with olives.

Serves 4

Time-saver

SAVE A CHILLING WAIT

Keep salad ingredients (canned fish, meats, etc.) in the refrigerator, so they'll be ready-chilled when you want them.

For other salads (meat, fish, chicken, etc.), see Index.

Biscuits, Muffins, Bread

Biscuits

BISCUITS—BASIC RECIPE

1/8 teaspoon salt	3/4 cup milk
1/2 teaspoon sugar	2 cups biscuit mix

Start oven pre-heating to hot, or 450°F. Add sugar and salt to milk; pour into biscuit mix and mix with a fork only until well combined. No need to roll biscuits out. Simply spoon off walnut-size pieces and drop onto a lightly greased pie tin or cookie sheet. Bake 10 to 15 minutes or until nicely browned.

18 min.

Note: To make a half-recipe of biscuits, use half the ingredients. Half of 3/4 cup milk equals 6 tablespoons or 1/3 cup plus 2 teaspoons.

Makes 10 to 16

DROP YOUR BISCUITS

Time-saver

There's no reason for *you* to do it, merely because your mother and grandmother took the extra time and used the extra energy to roll and cut biscuits. Make dropped biscuits instead and be through with your baking work in minutes.

If you insist on making rolled biscuits, roll the dough out to a square or rectangle; use a sharp knife to cut *square* biscuits. That way you'll save having to gather up and roll out again the scraps left by round-cutting.

A DROPPED BISCUIT DECORATIVE TRICK

Hint

After placing biscuits on baking pan, "fluff" the tops a little by pulling up dough with the points of a sharp-tined fork. Biscuits bake with attractive extra-brown "spines" on top.

BACON BISCUITS

20 min.

Prepare basic biscuit recipe above. Crumble 2 handfuls cocktail bacon rind snacks into fine bits; add ⅛ teaspoon salt to improve the flavor and toss to combine. Drop biscuits into bacon mixture; then place bacon side up on baking pan. Bake as directed.

Makes 10 to 16

CHEESE BISCUITS

18 min.

To basic biscuit recipe above add ⅓ cup grated Parmesan, Romano, or American cheese, before adding liquid. Stir cheese through mix, then add liquid and proceed as directed.

Makes 10 to 16

CHEESE BISCUITS—VARIATIONS

Flatten tops of dropped biscuits made *without* cheese by pressing lightly with a spoon. Dab tops with a little milk, using your finger tip, then sprinkle lightly with grated cheese. Bake.

Use a sharp knife point to gouge out small holes in the tops of dropped biscuits made *without* cheese. Tuck a bit of jar cheese in hole, "blue" cheese flavor preferred.

FRYING PAN BISCUITS

20 min.

Prepare basic biscuit recipe above. In a large heavy skillet melt two tablespoons butter. Spoon in walnut-size biscuits, leaving a little space between them. Cover skillet snugly and cook over low heat for 15 minutes. Biscuits are done when tops are firm and dry. Excellent with scrambled or sunnyside eggs.

Makes 10 to 16

HERB BISCUITS

Hint

Your fancy is your guide. To basic biscuit recipe (above) or Sour Cream Biscuits (see Index) add ½ teaspoon sage, curry powder, poppy, celery or caraway seeds, dehydrated celery, onion, or parsley flakes. Herb biscuits go well with bland, creamed dishes.

HONEY BISCUITS

20 min.

Bake basic biscuit recipe above. When biscuits are done, dip top half-inch first in melted butter, then in thick clover honey. Turn right side up and serve at once. Try these with scrambled eggs and sausages!

Makes 10 to 16

HORS D'OEUVRES BISCUITS

20 min.

Use half the basic biscuit recipe above. Mix as directed. Spoon off thimble-size pieces. Dab the top of each biscuit with a bit of anchovy paste. Bake at 400°F. for 10 minutes or until done.

Makes about 36

20 min.

JAM BISCUITS

Prepare basic biscuit recipe above. Lightly flatten tops of dropped biscuits by pressing lightly with a spoon. Gouge out a small hole in the top of each biscuit, using a sharp knife point; fill hole with a strawberry or cherry from jam. Dribble a little jam over tops of biscuits. Bake 10 to 15 minutes or until nicely browned.

Makes 10 to 16

20 min.

MINCEMEAT BISCUITS

Prepare basic biscuit recipe above. When batter is mixed, add 3 tablespoons or more canned or bottled ready-to-use mincemeat and combine thoroughly. Add 3 or 4 minutes baking time.

Makes 10 to 16

20 min.

SALT-TOP BISCUITS

Prepare basic biscuit recipe above, or, better, Sour Cream Biscuits below. Slightly flatten tops of dropped biscuits by pressing with a spoon; dab tops with milk, using your finger tip. Sprinkle sparingly with coarse salt crystals and a few caraway seeds (or celery salt, if desired). Bake as directed.

Makes 10 to 16

20 min.

APPLE BUTTER BISCUITS

Prepare basic biscuit recipe above. Slightly flatten tops of dropped biscuits with a spoon; gouge out a small hole in each, using a sharp knife point. Fill hole with apple butter and spread apple butter over the top. Bake as directed.

Makes 10 to 16

FRUIT BISCUITS

20 min.

1 recipe biscuits (see basic recipe above)
½ cup canned fruit cocktail
6 maraschino cherries, chopped
2 drops lemon extract

Dredge drained fruit cocktail and cherries through dry mix. Add lemon extract to milk and proceed as directed in recipe.

Note: In place of fruit cocktail use ½ cup glacé fruit, chopped, or fruitcake fruit (the kind packed in small cans or glass jars).

Makes 10 to 16

SOUR CREAM BISCUITS

18 min.

⅛ teaspoon salt
½ teaspoon sugar
⅓ cup milk plus 1 tablespoon
⅓ cup sour cream
2 cups biscuit mix

Start oven pre-heating to hot or 450°. Add sugar and salt to milk; add sour cream and mix well. Pour liquid into biscuit mix and mix with a fork only until well combined. Spoon off walnut-size pieces and drop onto a lightly greased pie tin or cookie sheet. Bake 10 to 15 minutes or until nicely browned. Makes an unusually rich and flaky biscuit, excellent for topping meat or chicken pie, or for just plain good eating!

Makes 10 to 16

DE LUXE BISCUITS

20 min.

⅛ teaspoon salt
½ teaspoon sugar
2 cups biscuit mix
3 tablespoons softened butter
⅔ cup milk

Start oven pre-heating to 450°. Stir sugar and salt through biscuit mix. Add butter (margarine may be used) and work mix with your fingers until mealy. Add milk. Mix with a fork only until well combined. Spoon off walnut-size pieces and drop onto a lightly greased pie tin or cookie sheet. Bake 10 to 15 minutes or until nicely browned.

Makes 10 to 16

CREAM CHEESE BISCUITS

20 min.

- milk
- 1 3-oz. package cream cheese
- ½ teaspoon sugar
- ⅛ teaspoon salt
- 2 cups biscuit mix

Start oven pre-heating to 450°. Beat ⅓ cup milk and cheese until smooth; add milk to make ¾ cup liquid. Add sugar and salt to milk; pour into biscuit mix, and mix with a fork only until well combined. Spoon off walnut-size pieces and drop onto a lightly greased pie tin or cookie sheet. Bake 10 to 15 minutes or until nicely browned.

Note: These make an excellent hors d'oeuvre base when baked thimble-size as in Hors D'oeuvres Biscuits (see above). Split the biscuits while hot, spread with fish or meat paste and put together again to form tiny sandwiches.

Makes 10 to 16

Ready-to-Bake Biscuits (Canned)

BISCUIT KNOTS

15 min.

Pre-heat oven to hot. Roll ready-to-bake canned biscuits between palms of hands until pencil-shaped and about 6 inches long; tie into a simple knot; dip top of each knot in celery salt sprinkled into a saucer. Bake as directed on package.

Serves 6 to 8

CHEESE STICKS

20 min.

Pre-heat oven to hot. Use ready-to-bake canned biscuits. Cut each biscuit in half; roll each half between palms of hands to pencil diameter. Cut "pencils" in half; dip each end first in milk or water, then in grated cheese. Bake as directed on package.

Note: These are excellent for hors d'oeuvres.

Makes about 40

QUICK CHEESE BISCUITS

18 min.

Pre-heat oven to hot. Generously spread the tops of ready-to-bake canned biscuits with jar cheese, any flavor. Or spread Biscuit Knots (see above). Bake as directed on the package.

Serves 6 to 8

CLOVERLEAF BISCUITS

15 to 18 min.

Pre-heat oven to hot. Roll ready-to-bake canned biscuits between palms of hands to make short, fat cigars; cut into thirds; roll each third into a ball. Stick three balls together; bake as directed on package.

Serves 6 to 8

MINIATURE CLOVERLEAVES—VARIATION

These are "two-bite" size. Cut biscuits in half; roll each half between palms to make a slender cigar.

Cut each cigar into thirds; roll into balls. Stick three balls together; bake as directed on package.

Note: For another variation see Poppy Seed Biscuits (below).

15 min.

CURRY BISCUITS

Pre-heat oven to hot. Combine 1/4 teaspoon or very slightly more curry powder with 1/4 cup fine bread crumbs. Moisten tops of ready-to-bake biscuits with your finger dipped in milk or water; dip biscuit tops into bread crumb mixture. Bake as directed on package.

Serves 6 to 8

15 min.

ONION BISCUITS

Pre-heat oven to hot. Moisten tops of ready-to-bake canned biscuits with your finger dipped in milk or water. Evenly spread a few bits of finely chopped onion on each biscuit. Bake as directed on package.

Serves 6 to 8

15 min.

POPPY SEED BISCUITS

Pre-heat oven to hot. Moisten tops of ready-to-bake canned biscuits with finger dipped in milk or water. Sprinkle a generous pinch of poppy seeds over each biscuit. Bake as directed on package. Cloverleaf Biscuits (above) may also be made this way.

Serves 6 to 8

BISCUIT ROLL-UPS OR POCKETBOOKS

- 1 can ready-to-bake biscuits
- 2 tablespoons flour
- filling ingredients (see below)

20 min.

Pre-heat oven to hot. Measure flour into a saucer; dip both sides of biscuits in flour and shake off excess. Place biscuits on waxed paper and roll into rough ovals, about 1/4 inch thick (a smooth-sided water tumbler makes a quickie rolling pin). Add filling as recipes direct, leaving a 1-inch margin all around the edge of the biscuit.

TO SHAPE FILLED ROLL-UPS

Moisten edge all around with your finger dipped in water. Starting at a wide edge, roll up tightly, like a jelly roll; pinch seam and ends of roll to seal. Arrange on lightly greased cookie sheet or pie tin, seam sides up.

TO SHAPE FILLED POCKETBOOKS

Make a deep crease across center of oval, using the back of a kitchen knife. Arrange filling on one half, leaving a margin around edge. Moisten edge of other half with your finger dipped in water. Fold over; pinch edge to seal. Arrange on lightly greased cookie sheet or pie tin.

TO BAKE ROLL-UPS OR POCKETBOOKS

Bake for time directed on package, or until nicely browned.

Serves 6 to 8

CHEESE ROLL-UPS

See above for method. Place a finger of Cheddar or American cheese on each oval.

BLUE CHEESE ROLL-UPS

See above for method. Spread ovals with blue-cheese flavor jar cheese (or any other flavor you prefer).

HAM OR BEEF ROLL-UPS

See above for method. Place a generous pinch of chopped cooked ham or shredded dried beef in center of each oval. (For an easy way to shred dried beef see Timesaver Index.)

MINCEMEAT ROLL-UPS

See above for method. Spread each oval with about 2 teaspoons ready-to-use canned- or jar-packed mincemeat. For a less tart flavor, sprinkle mincemeat with a little granulated sugar.

PEANUT BUTTER ROLL-UPS

See above for method. Spread ovals with peanut butter (the "chunky" style is best). For more flavor, sprinkle peanut butter with the merest speck of salt.

RAISIN ROLL-UPS

See above for method. On each oval spread a bit of softened butter; sprinkle over ½ teaspoon brown sugar; add a few raisins.

FRUIT POCKETBOOK BISCUITS

See above for method. On half of each oval place 2 teaspoons glacé fruitcake fruit, or well-drained fruit salad.

HERB POCKETBOOK BISCUITS

See above for method. Place a bean-size bit of butter on half of each oval. Sprinkle sparingly with the herb of your choice: sage, parsley, caraway seeds, dehydrated onion or celery flakes.

OTHER POCKETBOOK BISCUITS

See roll-up recipes above: Cheese, Ham or Beef, Mincemeat, or Raisin. Use ingredients given; shape biscuits as pocketbooks.

Muffins

CORN MUFFINS

20 min.

- 1 generous cup corn muffin mix
- ¼ cup milk
- 1 egg yolk
- a tiny pinch of salt

Note: For richer muffins, add 2 teaspoons melted butter.

Pre-heat oven to 375°. Beat milk, egg yolk and salt together lightly; add to muffin mix and stir into a smooth batter. Stir in butter if used. Spoon into 2 inch muffin cups lined with paper liners; bake 15 to 18 minutes or until done.

Makes 8 2-inch muffins

CORN MUFFINS—VARIATIONS

CORN NUT MUFFINS: Dredge ½ cup chopped almonds and a handful of seedless raisins through mix, before adding liquid.

HERB CORN MUFFINS: Add herbs of your choice to batter: 1 teaspoon dehydrated parsley or celery flakes; 1/4 teaspoon dehydrated onion flakes; a pinch of oregano or sage.

CORN-BEEF MUFFINS: Omit salt from recipe. Add 1/4 cup finely shredded dried chipped beef to batter. See above for an easy way to shred chipped beef.

CORN-CORN MUFFINS: Add to batter up to 1/2 cup cooked kernel-style corn, well drained.

APPLE CORN MUFFINS: Add to batter 1/2 cup "pie apples." Or make muffins as directed in basic recipe; top each with a teaspoon of apple butter before baking.

JAM CORN MUFFINS: After turning batter into muffin cups, push a strawberry or cherry from jam down into each muffin.

Bakery Corn Muffins

15 min.

HONEY BUTTER CORN MUFFINS

Cut small wedges from the tops of bakery corn muffins, using a sharp pointed knife. Drop in a little honey and a bit of butter. Cut off wedge tops and replace on muffins. Heat in a moderate oven for about 10 minutes.

15 min.

SURPRISE CORN MUFFINS

Cut a quarter-inch slice from tops of bakery corn muffins. Dig out a little cavity (use your fingers) and fill with strawberry or cherry jam. Dribble a little jam over cut edge, replace top. Heat in a moderate oven for about 10 minutes.

CHEESE CORN MUFFINS

10 min.

Spread tops of bakery corn muffins with softened butter, then with sharp jar cheese. Place in hot oven for 5 to 8 minutes. Or, *faster:* prepare muffins as directed and place under hot broiler heat for 2 or 3 minutes.

6 muffins serve 4 to 6

English Muffins

APPLE ENGLISH MUFFINS

10 min.

Split English muffins and toast lightly. Butter, then spread generously with apple butter; sprinkle with grated cheese. Place under hot broiler for a few moments.

Timesaver: When toasting muffins for a crowd, do it under the broiler and make several at a time.

4 muffins serve 3 or 4

CHEESE ENGLISH MUFFINS

10 min.

Split and toast muffins lightly. Butter, then spread generously with any flavor jar cheese. Brown under hot broiler heat for 2 or 3 minutes. Place a spoonful of strawberry or cherry jam in the center of each before serving.

4 muffins serve 3 or 4

EASY ENGLISH MUFFIN SERVICE

Hint

When you're going to be so busy in the kitchen you won't have time to toast English muffins, cut them across into 3/4 inch slices. Pile into a pie tin and place in a hot oven. In about 15 minutes they'll be crisp on the outside, tender and hot on the inside.

Bread

To serve hot breads, rolls, or biscuits, use a wicker bread basket, or a well-warmed deep serving dish. Lay two snowy-white dinner napkins over the dish, toss in baked article hot as can be from the oven. Pick up one corner of one napkin at a time and fold over top of dish.

If you can get to an Italian bakery, serve those long crusty loaves as often as possible. They *taste* good, and there's nothing better for adding "dress" to your table. Just pop the loaf into a hot oven for 5 minutes or so, or until heated through. Break into chunks to serve.

DOUBLE-QUICK BROWN-AND-SERVE FRENCH BREAD

Time-saver

Cut loaf in half the long way. Place cut sides down under hot broiler heat for 2 or 3 minutes or until lightly toasted; then turn bread over and lightly toast cut sides. Break into chunks to serve.

DOUBLE-QUICK BROWN-AND-SERVE FRENCH BREAD, GARLIC STYLE

Time-saver

Cut bread in half the long way; place cut sides down under broiler heat until lightly browned. Remove from oven and butter cut sides.

For pronounced garlic flavor: toast buttered sides under broiler until brown, then rub lightly with a cut clove of garlic.

For milder garlic flavor: rub buttered surfaces with cut clove of garlic before toasting.

CHEESE FRENCH BREAD

15 to 18 min.

1 long loaf French or Italian bread

jar cheese, or sharp cheese slices

Method I: Spread top of loaf lightly with softened butter, then jar cheese. Place in hot oven until nicely browned.

Method II: Make deep diagonal slashes in loaf, almost to bottom crust. Slip slices of sharp cheese into cuts. Place in hot oven until browned.

Note: May be made with brown-and-serve or regular French or Italian bread.

1 small loaf serves 4

ONION FRENCH BREAD

1 egg yolk
2 tablespoons water

1 loaf brown-and-serve French bread
small onion

15 to 18 min.

Beat egg yolk with water and brush on top of bread. Cut onion into paper thin slices; pull slices into rings and spread rings lightly on loaf. Or make about 2 tablespoons chopped onion and sprinkle over loaf. Brown as directed on the package, adding a few extra minutes.

1 small loaf serves 2 or 3

15 to 18 min.

BROWN-AND-SERVE ONION ROLLS

Beat an egg yolk with 2 tablespoons water. Brush tops of rolls with egg mixture, then dip tops into very finely chopped onions. Brown as directed on the package; add a few extra minutes of time.

6 rolls serve 4

Hint

"SALT" RYE BREAD

Many stores now carry rye bread, baked in long, slim loaves for cocktail snacks. It goes wonderfully with creamed dishes or soups. To serve: Wrap the loaf in aluminum foil and place in a hot oven for 10 minutes or so, until heated through. Serve with unsalted butter.

Time-saver

QUICK FRENCH TOAST

Make French Toast with *French* Bread—the long "skinny" loaves. You can crowd more of the small-size slices into your skillet, hence cook more portions at a time and serve *more* people in less time.

20 min.

FRENCH TOAST

2 eggs
¼ cup cream
¾ cup milk
1 tablespoon sugar, or slightly less
⅛ teaspoon nutmeg
a pinch of salt
8 slices bread

Beat eggs, liquid and seasonings together, using a rotary beater. Pour over bread slices arranged in a shallow dish. Turn slices a few times, until they will absorb no more liquid. Fry in a hot skillet, in plenty of butter, 6 to 8 minutes to a side, or until nicely browned. Top each slice with a fried egg and crisp bacon, or scrambled eggs and browned canned breakfast sausages, or serve plain with syrup or jam on the side.

8 slices serve 4 to 6

DESSERT FRENCH TOAST

20 min.

Allow two thin slices French bread for each serving. Add 2 tablespoons of sugar and ½ teaspoon vanilla extract to the liquid. When ready to serve, sprinkle with confectioner's sugar, and place a generous spoonful of marmalade, strawberry, or other jam on the center of each slice. If desired, add to the liquid a tablespoon of cognac or kirsch.

HOW TO SLICE BREAD "PAPER"-THIN FOR HORS D'OEUVRES

Time-saver

Use unsliced bread. Turn loaf up on its end, spread the cut surface, and then slice the bread as thin as you like. A good bread saw helps.

"FIRST-BUTTERED" TOAST

10 min.

This toast should not be made in an electric toaster. Slice bread ½ inch thick, and place under hot broiler heat until one side is toasted. Remove and butter untoasted side generously; return to broiler butter side up. When brown and bubbly, serve with jam.

6 slices serve 4

HOW TO FRESHEN A STALE LOAF

Hint

Lightly moisten top and bottom crusts with a few drops of water. Wrap loaf tightly in aluminum foil and heat for 15 minutes in a 400° oven.

SIZZLING CINNAMON TOAST

10 min.

See "First-Buttered" Toast above. When buttered side of bread is lightly browned, remove from broiler, sprinkle with cinnamon sugar (1/4 cup of sugar mixed with 1 teaspoon cinnamon). Return to broiler until nicely browned; serve at once.

Cakes

There's no better timesaver for cake-loving families than ready-baked un-iced sponge layers. Anything you might do with cake you've baked yourself you can do, and deliciously, with these cakes. Top them with sauce, ice them with puddings, serve them warmed, merely sprinkled with powdered sugar as a fruit accompaniment, or ice with your favorite frosting.

Sponge cake layers are economical, too, allowing you really to splurge on the accompaniment.

QUICK COCONUT CAKE

1 recipe Vanilla Frosting (see Index)
2 8-inch sponge cake layers
shredded moist coconut

Prepare frosting as directed. Reserve ½ cup. Ice top of one cake layer and sprinkle generously with coconut. Add second layer and frost top. Thin reserved frosting with another teaspoon of liquid until not quite runny. Spread thinned frosting on sides of cake and use any leftover on top. Sprinkle coconut on top and sides of cake (see Timesaver Index for an easy way to put coconut on the sides of a cake).

15 to 20 min.

Serves 6 to 8

PACKAGED PUDDINGS MAKE QUICK, TASTY LAYER FILLINGS

Hint

Any flavor cooked or uncooked pudding dessert may be used for layer fillings, with tasty results. Follow basic recipe for pudding (see Index); allow to cool slightly before spreading over cake.

One 4-oz. package of pudding mix makes plenty for four layers. For two-layer cakes make half a pudding recipe, or make the whole recipe and use left-over pudding for lunch dessert or snacks.

12 min.

COCONUT-CREAM CAKE

- 1 recipe Coconut-Cream Pudding (see Index)
- 4-oz. can moist coconut
- 2 8-inch sponge cake layers

Prepare pudding as directed. After removing from heat, stir in about 1/3 of the can of coconut. Spread hot pudding on a cake layer, add second layer, spread thickly with more pudding and let it run down cake sides. Sprinkle top generously with half or more of the remaining coconut. Serve at once.

Serves 6 to 8

15 min.

SAUCE CAKE

- 1 recipe Vanilla or Chocolate Pudding (see Index)
- 1 egg yolk
- 2 8-inch sponge cake layers

Prepare pudding as directed, beating egg yolk into liquid before cooking. Meanwhile slice cake layers in two and pile slices on each other to make a 4-layer cake. Cut into 8 equal serving wedges. Take off top layer of wedges and arrange on a serving plate in the shape of the original cake. Spoon hot pudding over generously; add another layer of wedges and repeat, until cake is reconstructed. Spoon pudding over top; sprinkle with chopped nuts and serve at once.

Note: Cake may be made without first cutting into

wedges, but it is much easier to serve if prepared as directed, since the sponge layers are quite fragile.

Serves 6 to 8

SAUCE CAKE—VARIATIONS

ORANGE: When vanilla pudding has cooked, stir in 3 tablespoons orange juice, 1/4 teaspoon orange extract. Top cake with spoonfuls of orange marmalade instead of nuts.

FIG: Add 4 teaspoons lemon juice to a 16-oz. jar preserved figs, mix, and let stand while cutting cake. Drain off fig syrup and reserve for another dish. Set aside 4 figs for top of cake; slightly crush remainder, and spread on second layer of cake. Place one fig-half on top of each portion of completed cake. (This takes about 5 minutes longer to make.)

15 min.

APRICOT: Add 1 teaspoon lemon juice to one No. 2 can apricots; proceed as directed for fig variation, dicing apricots, rather than crushing.

DOUBLE BOSTON CREAM PIE: Spread cake layers as directed in Sauce Cake. Omit pudding from top of cake. Sprinkle generously with confectioner's sugar.

EASY WHOLE NUT MEATS

Time-saver

Before cracking Brazil nuts, place in boiling water for 5 minutes. Drain, cool, and crack shell without crushing kernel. The nut meat will come out whole. Prepare a few handfuls of nuts this way and keep tightly covered on your kitchen shelf, for use whenever nuts are called for. Two or three Brazil nut kernels make plenty of nut chips for a garnish. Be sure nuts are completely dry before storing.

SPICY MOCHA NUT CAKE

- milk
- 1 egg yolk
- ½ teaspoon soluble coffee, dissolved in 1 tablespoon boiling water
- 1 package butterscotch pudding mix
- ⅛ teaspoon each, cinnamon and ginger
- a tiny pinch of cloves
- 2 8-inch sponge cake layers
- chopped nuts

18 min.

Measure out milk to amount directed on pudding package, beat in egg yolk; add coffee. Add pudding mix and spices; mix; cook as directed on package. When pudding is ready, spread hot over one cake layer, sprinkle lightly with nuts; add second layer and spread with more pudding, allowing pudding to run down sides. Sprinkle top generously with chopped nuts. Serve at once.

Serves 4 to 6

NUT-TOPPING FOR CAKE— THAT STAYS PUT!

Time-saver

Ice cake with frosting of your choice, reserving about ½ cup. Thin frosting with a little more liquid until it is about the consistency of very thick molasses. Spread thinned frosting over sides and top of cake; sprinkle with nuts (or coconut); pat gently and the topping will stick.

TO OVEN-HEAT CAKE WITHOUT SCORCHING

Hint

Place cake in a lightly buttered pan inside another pan which contains a half-inch of hot water in the bottom. Heat in moderate oven.

CHOCOLATE CAKE

- 2 or 3 cream-center dark-chocolate-covered candy bars
- 2 8-inch sponge cake layers
- 3 tablespoons confectioner's sugar, sifted
- 1 teaspoon cocoa, sifted
- a tiny pinch of nutmeg

15 min.

Start oven pre-heating to slow. Cut candy bars into ¼ inch slices and arrange candy evenly over *one* cake layer. Place both layers in oven for 5 to 10 minutes, or until candy is melted. (Candy bar slices may not *look* melted. To test, touch slices with a knife blade; if they spread, they're melted and ready.) Meanwhile combine sugar, cocoa, and nutmeg. When candy is melted, spread it with the flat of a knife over the one layer; add second layer. Sprinkle top with cocoa mixture (see Hint Index, Fancy Sugar Dress for Cake, for a handsome way to do it), and serve.

Timesaver: Cover both layers. Place in oven as directed. Spread both layers and put together as a layer cake. Omit sprinkling with cocoa. Top with chopped nuts, if desired.

Serves 6 to 8

MOCHA CHOCOLATE CAKE

- ¼ teaspoon soluble coffee, dissolved in 1 teaspoon boiling water
- 2 teaspoons milk
- 4 cream-center dark-chocolate-covered candy bars
- 2 8-inch sponge cake layers
- chopped nuts or coconut

10 min.

Prepare coffee in a small saucepan. Add milk and candy bars, broken into chunks. Cook and stir over low heat until combined; if too thick, add milk by quarter-teaspoons to thin, stirring well after each addition. Spread "icing" over a cake layer, add second layer and spread remainder over top, reserving a little for the sides. Sprinkle with chopped nuts or a little coconut.

Serves 6 to 8

BITTERSWEET CAKE

2 tablespoons cocoa
3 tablespoons sugar
⅓ cup milk
⅓ cup chocolate syrup
a pinch of nutmeg
¼ teaspoon vanilla extract
1 9-oz. pound-cake loaf
½ cup heavy cream
½ teaspoon sugar
⅛ teaspoon vanilla extract

15 min.

Combine first five ingredients in a saucepan and simmer 5 minutes. Remove from heat and stir in ¼ teaspoon vanilla. Meanwhile cut cake into 1-inch cubes, and whip cream very stiff, adding ½ teaspoon sugar and vanilla. To serve: dip cake cubes into sauce, arrange 4 or more to a portion in dessert saucers, spoon more chocolate sauce over. Top with whipped cream.

Serves 4 to 6

PRUNE SPICE CAKE

1 8-oz. jar "junior" baby food prunes
¼ teaspoon cinnamon
⅛ teaspoon ginger
a pinch of cloves
¼ teaspoon lemon extract
milk
1 package vanilla pudding
2 8-inch sponge cake layers

12 min.

Turn prunes into measuring cup. Add spices and extract, combine; add milk to make quantity of liquid called for on pudding package; turn into saucepan, add pudding, combine well and cook as directed on package. Spread a cake layer with hot pudding, add second layer, spoon on more pudding, letting it run down over sides. If desired, garnish top with a few canned apricots, diced.

Serves 6 to 8

TART APPLE CAKE

10 min

1 10-oz. jar apple jelly
2 level tablespoons vanilla instant pudding mix (uncooked type)
2 8-inch sponge cake layers
ready-whipped topping

Turn jelly into a bowl and beat vigorously with a rotary beater until it looks like butterscotch. Add pudding mix and stir until well combined. Spread one cake layer lightly with jelly mixture, pipe ready-whipped topping around edge. Spread second layer with remainder of jelly and place on first. Decorate generously with topping.

Serves 6 to 8

APPLE BUTTER CAKE

15 min.

1 cup heavy cream
1 teaspoon sugar
¼ teaspoon vanilla extract
a tiny pinch of salt
¼ cup apple butter
2 8-inch sponge cake layers
coconut

Whip cream very stiff, adding sugar and vanilla. Stir salt into apple butter and gently fold into whipped cream. Spread one layer of cake lightly with cream mixture; add second layer; spread top and sides. Sprinkle top generously with coconut.

Serves 6 to 8

APPLE TOAST

18 min.

1 9-oz. pound cake loaf, un-iced
1 #2 can apple sauce
butter
cinnamon sugar

Cut cake into half-inch or thicker slices; place under a medium hot broiler and lightly toast both sides. Butter one side lightly, sprinkle with cinnamon sugar and spread generously with apple sauce. Return to broiler for a minute or two. Serve at once in bowls with cream on the side.

Serves 6 or more

15 min.

APPLE TOAST—VARIATION

Toast one side of cake only. Spread untoasted side lightly with any flavor jar cheese. Place under broiler for 1 to 2 minutes, or until cheese bubbles slightly. Remove from heat, spread generously with apple sauce, sprinkle lightly with cinnamon sugar, and return to broiler for a minute or two.

10 min.

APPLESAUCE SANDWICHES

- ¼ cup crumbled blue cheese
- 1½ cups tart applesauce (see Note)
- 1 9-oz. pound cake loaf
- whipped cream or ready-whipped topping

Stir cheese into applesauce. Slice cake very thin. Make triple-decker sandwiches, using applesauce mixture as a filling. Pile whipped cream, made with but a trace of sweetening, or ready-whipped topping over sandwiches.

Note: If applesauce is sweet, stir in 1 teaspoon lemon juice.

Serves 4

15 min.

QUICK UPSIDE-DOWN CAKE

- 4 to 6 tablespoons sugar
- 5 teaspoons cornstarch, dissolved in 1 tablespoon water
- ⅛ teaspoon lemon extract
- 1 drop almond extract
- 1 teaspoon lemon juice
- 1 #2 can fruit (sliced peaches, diced apricots, or cherries)
- 1 8-inch sponge cake layer

Start oven pre-heating to medium. Combine all ingredients, except cake, in a saucepan; use 4 tablespoons sugar for sweet fruit, more if tart. Cook and stir over low heat until mixture clears and thickens. Turn into an 8-inch cake pan, spread evenly, place cake on top; place in oven for 5 to 8 minutes, or until well warmed. To serve: place serving plate face down on cake, grasp cake pan (which will be hot!) and plate and turn over. Lift off pan. If desired, serve in deep dishes, with heavy cream on the side.

Serves 6 to 8

LEFTOVER CAKE DESSERT

Hint

Use ingredients and method in Chocolate Meringues (see Index), but use half-inch slices of leftover cake instead of shortcake cups as directed in recipe. Trim cake slices into squares and remove frosting from top and sides.

CAKE SANDWICHES

15 min.

3-oz. package cream cheese
heavy cream
3 tablespoons sifted confectioner's sugar
1 9-oz. pound cake loaf, un-iced
strawberry jam
ready-whipped topping

Thin cheese with 2 tablespoons cream, add sugar, and work into a smooth paste. Trim one end of cake smooth. Spread trimmed surface of cake with a little cheese mixture; cut off as thin a slice as possible and lay it cheese side up. Spread cut surface of cake again with cheese, cut off another thin slice and place cheese side up on first. Now cut off a thin slice of plain cake and place it on cake slices to make a triple-decker. Make 4 sandwiches, or more if needed. Coat top and sides of each sandwich with jam; decorate tops with whipped topping.

Note: This dessert may be "stretched" by cutting each sandwich in half, to make twice the quantity.

Serves 4 or more

CREAM CHEESE CAKE

15 min.

- 2 3-oz. packages cream cheese
- 4 or 5 tablespoons milk
- tiny pinch of salt
- 3 tablespoons sifted confectioner's sugar
- 2 8-inch sponge cake layers
- cinnamon sugar

Mix cheese and milk together until smooth and thin enough to spread easily. Add salt and sugar; mix well. Reserve ⅓ cup. Slice cakes across to make 4 layers. Spread a layer with cheese, sprinkle lightly with cinnamon sugar, add another layer and spread it, and so on until all the layers have been used. Spread top generously and sprinkle with cinnamon sugar. Ice sides of cake with reserved frosting thinned with a little more milk. Sprinkle cinnamon sugar on sides.

Serves 6 to 8

CREAM CHEESE CAKE—VARIATIONS

15 min.

BRANDY: Add ½ teaspoon brandy extract to cheese mixture.

RUM: Thin apple jelly with dark rum and spread cake layers very lightly with mixture before spreading with cheese, or, add ½ teaspoon rum flavoring to cream cheese mixture.

BLACK-WALNUT: Add ¼ teaspoon black walnut extract to cheese mixture. Stir in ¼ cup chopped walnuts, if desired.

FIG: Before starting cheese mixture, coarsely chop 6 or 8 canned figs and turn into a bowl containing 2 teaspoons lemon juice. Mix. When cake is ready, drain figs and spread over top of cake. Omit cinnamon sugar. Top with puffs of whipped cream.

DON'T FORGET LADYFINGERS

Hints

Most recipes using sponge cake layers as a base can be made with ladyfingers. To serve as a loaf, split strips of ladyfingers as they come from the package, using halves as layers. For best results, don't make desserts more than two ladyfingers thick.

If you prefer to serve individual portions of a ladyfinger dessert, it's quicker to make it as a loaf, reserving a little topping or filling. Pull ladyfingers into portions, using two forks; transfer to serving plates. Spoon reserved topping or filling over each portion.

Easiest ladyfinger desserts to make are those using packaged puddings as fillings or toppings.

Note: For more ladyfinger serving ideas, see Bakery or Leftover Un-iced Cup Cakes (Index).

FRUIT-TOPPED SHORTCAKE SHELLS

(Prepare this before starting dinner)

5 min.

4 sponge cake shortcake shells
apple or currant jelly
1 package frozen fruit (peaches, sliced strawberries, or other berries)
ready-whipped topping

Lightly spread insides of shells with jelly. Using a sharp pointed knife, break fruit into small chunks; place spoonfuls of fruit in each shell and set aside.

When dessert time rolls around, fruit will have thawed. Garnish each portion with puffs of topping.

Note: Canned fruit may be used, if desired, in which case place well-drained fruit in shells just before serving.

Serves 4

18 min.

MINCEMEAT SHELLS

½ cup or more can- or jar-packed mincemeat
4 sponge cake shortcake shells
cheese wedges, or 1 recipe Rum Sauce (see Index)

Start broiler pre-heating to medium low. Pile mincemeat into shells; dot generously with butter. Place under broiler 3 or 4 minutes or until piping hot. Watch carefully. Serve on dessert plates with cheese wedges on the side. Top with sauce.

Note: Taste mincemeat. If too tart, add 2 or 3 teaspoons sugar and mix well before placing in shells.

Serves 4

20 min.

BERRY HILL (Quick Fruit Shortcake)

½ recipe Biscuits—Basic Recipe (see Index)
2 teaspoons sugar
1 cup heavy cream
2 teaspoons sugar
½ teaspoon vanilla extract
1 #2 can berries (strawberries, raspberries, loganberries, etc.,) or frozen berries, thawed.

To biscuit mix add two teaspoons sugar and prepare as directed, making dropped biscuits. Bake for minimum time, or until just done. Cut hot biscuits into eighths and spread out to cool. Meanwhile whip cream very stiff, adding the second 2 teaspoons sugar and vanilla extract. Drain berries well. To serve:

place half the biscuit pieces in bottom of a deep bowl. Spoon half the berries over, add all the whipped cream, then remaining biscuits, then remaining fruit. Gently fold all together until just combined. Pile into a hill on serving dish and serve at once.

Timesaver: Shape biscuits no bigger than thimbles and use them as baked, without cutting (allow biscuits to cool before adding whipped cream).

Serves 6 to 8

LEFTOVER CAKE "SHORTCAKE"

5 min.

4 half-inch slices cake
⅓ cup light cream
1 #2 can fruit, any variety
ready-whipped topping

If cake is iced, remove icing. Mix cream with a few tablespoons of syrup from fruit. Arrange cake on serving plates; spoon cream-syrup mixture over, until well moistened. Pile with well-drained fruit, and puff topping on generously. Garnish with a few bits of fruit.

Serves 4

QUICK CRUMBCAKE DESSERT

10 min.

1 bakery crumbcake
cinnamon sugar
1 #2 can apricots
heavy cream, plain or whipped and lightly sweetened

Sprinkle top of cake lightly with cinnamon sugar and place in moderate oven to warm. Meanwhile drain apricots and turn fruit into a saucepan. Crush slightly with a fork. Place over low heat and warm fruit. To serve: cut cake into squares, place in deep bowls, and spoon fruit over. Pour on cream. Or, leave cake whole, top with fruit, and at the last minute before serving, top with whipped cream.

Serves 6 to 8

RUM ROLL

confectioner's sugar
1 6-inch jelly roll
½ cup apple jelly
¼ teaspoon rum (or brandy) extract
ready-whipped topping, or stiffly whipped cream

10 min.

Sprinkle a 2-foot sheet of waxed paper generously with sugar. Place jelly roll at one end of sheet, seam side up. Break seam with a sharp knife and carefully unroll roll, using knife edge if cake sticks. (If cake is very thin, don't unroll last turn.) Meanwhile beat apple jelly with a rotary beater until it looks like butterscotch. Add extract, and beat again for a moment. Lightly brush or spread jelly over the jelly on cake, then spread very generously with ready-whipped topping (see Note). Roll cake up again, sprinkle top evenly with confectioner's sugar. Pull into serving pieces, using two forks.

Note: Ready-whipped topping may be used if cake is to be served at once. If cake is to stand for a bit, use stiffly whipped cream (see Index).

Serves 6

HOT RUMMY COFFEECAKE

1 coffee ring or 6 individual coffeecakes
Coffeecake Frosting (see Index)
rum extract

15 min.

Select un-iced coffeecake, preferably without filling. Wrap snugly in aluminum foil and place in a medium oven 5 to 7 minutes, or until well heated. Meanwhile prepare frosting as directed, using rum extract instead of vanilla. To serve: cut coffeering into serving portions, or individual pastries into quarters; arrange in original shape on serving plate. Dribble frosting over cakes, and be generous. Serve with jam or marmalade on the side, if desired.

Note: This is an excellent and filling dessert after a one dish dinner, especially if you've served a green salad.

Serves 6

Ice-Cream-and-Cake Desserts

Use sponge cake layers or sponge cake shortcake shells as bases for ice cream desserts. Take a little time to prepare your dessert—*anybody* can serve a piece of cake with a few spoonfuls of ice cream.

Serve either plenty of ice cream and a little cake, or the reverse, if you stick to the traditional "ice cream 'n cake" pattern. The two sweets should complement each other. Try to match or contrast flavors. For example, with a peach-flavored cake serve peach ice cream as a match, or with a pineapple-flavored cake serve strawberry ice cream as a contrast. Try serving chocolate-flavored desserts (or chocolate cake) with coffee ice cream instead of the conventional vanilla.

Hints

For desserts using ice cream slices, ask your ice cream dealer for *hard* brick ice cream and make sure you get it. It's far easier to handle.

Keep buffet-size cans of fruit or berries in the refrigerator to use as ice-cream-dessert makings. This size can contains just enough for 4.

For ice cream topping ideas, see Dessert Sauces (Index).

8 min.

QUICK ICE CREAM AND CAKE DESSERT

1 9-oz. pound cake loaf
1 pint brick ice cream
chocolate sauce, canned (or see Index)
ready-whipped topping

Trim cake to size of ice cream brick. Cut cake into very thin slices. Make 5-layer sandwiches: a slice of cake, a slice of ice cream, more cake, more ice cream, ending with cake. Top with a spoonful of chocolate sauce and a very generous puff of whipped topping.

Note: For best flavor use coffee ice cream.

Serves 4

5 min.

ICE CREAM FRUIT DESSERT

4 sponge cake shortcake shells
canned or frozen-thawed berries or fruit
vanilla or fruit-flavor ice cream
ready-whipped topping

Into each cake shell spoon fruit, well drained. Top with a generous spoonful of ice cream; spoon a little of the fruit syrup over the ice cream. Garnish with a puff of topping.

Serves 4

15 min.

ICE CREAM CRUMBCAKE

2 cups stale cake crumbs
1 pint brick ice cream
sundae sauce (see Index)
ready-whipped topping

Crumble cake into coarse crumbs and toast under medium broiler heat for 2 or 3 minutes. Spread crumbs out to cool. When cool, roll slices of ice cream in crumbs. Top each slice with a generous spoonful of sundae sauce and a generous puff of whipped topping.

Note: With *White* or *Yellow Cake* use vanilla,

cherry or strawberry ice cream; with *Spice Cake* use coffee ice cream; with *Chocolate Cake* use chocolate, vanilla, or coffee ice cream.

Serves 6

Fresh Home-Baked Cakes for 20-minute Cookery

Yes, you can do it—and the secret is *cupcakes.* Using a cake mix, you can have a batch of cupcakes in the oven within 5 minutes—and they'll be baked ready to eat, about 15 minutes later!

If you're using cake mixes for the first time, experiment with a different brand each time you bake, until you find just the one that satisfies you. It's all a matter of *your* personal taste, as it is with *any* packaged food.

Small cakes bake faster, so if you don't have one, buy yourself a two-inch cup muffin tin, and the paper liner cups that go with every well-dressed cupcake. (The paper cups save the time needed for greasing the cups, and make wash-up far easier!)

For toppings, see Hints—Bakery or Leftover Uniced Cupcakes (below), or mix up a quick frosting (see Index).

Note: Cakes should be cooled before icing with butter-type frostings.

CUPCAKES—BASIC RECIPE

20 min.

1 cup of cake mix
¼ cup milk
1 egg yolk
1 drop almond or lemon extract

Start oven pre-heating to 375°. Beat milk, egg,

and extract together, add to mix and beat until smooth (use a rotary beater). Half-fill muffin cups lined with paper liners. Bake 12 to 17 minutes or until a toothpick pushed into a cake comes out dry.

Cool slightly before removing paper cups, or serve in the cups.

Note: All measurements are level; do not pack cake mix into measuring cup.

Makes 8 two-inch cakes

CUPCAKES—VARIATIONS

CHOCOLATE: (From white-cake mix). Omit almond or lemon extract; add from 1 to 2 tablespoons of cocoa to dry mix; add ¼ teaspoon vanilla extract to liquid.

CHOCOLATE-CHUNK: Add a few tablespoons semi-sweet chocolate bits to batter after mixing; for *nut chocolate* cakes add ¼ cup nuts and chocolate.

SPICE: To dry mix add ¼ teaspoon cinnamon, ⅛ teaspoon each ginger and nutmeg, and a tiny pinch of cloves.

EGGNOG: To dry mix add ¼ teaspoon nutmeg; add one extra egg yolk and count it as part of liquid; sprinkle a pinch of nutmeg on top of each cake before baking.

NUT: To dry mix add ¼ cup or more chopped nuts; top each cake with a few bits of nut meats before baking.

MAPLENUT: Omit almond or lemon extract; add ¼ teaspoon maple flavoring and ¼ cup coarsely chopped walnuts to batter.

LEMON: Add 1/8 teaspoon lemon extract to milk; to dry mix add 1 teaspoon grated lemon rind or 1 tablespoon chopped fruitcake lemon peel.

ORANGE: As for lemon, substituting orange.

FRUIT: Add 2 tablespoons chopped fruitcake fruit, or 2 tablespoons well-drained fruit cocktail (canned).

TO MAKE A LARGER QUANTITY OF CUPCAKES

Hint

If you have a 16-cup cupcake tin, double Cupcakes—Basic Recipe (above), using 1 whole egg instead of 2 yolks.

TO STORE CAKE MIX

Hint

Keep unused mix in a glass jar, tightly covered. It will stay fresh and wholesome for several weeks.

WHAT TO DO WITH LEFTOVER EGG WHITES

Hint

Raw egg whites may be stored in a covered glass jar in the refrigerator, but not for more than two or three days.

If you have no immediate use for raw egg whites in other cookery, poach the white in gently boiling salt water for 10 minutes or so, until firm. Drain, and use it chopped, as garnish or salad ingredient.

BAKERY OR LEFTOVER UN-ICED CUPCAKES

Hints

Dip tops of cakes in canned chocolate sauce and sprinkle with chopped nuts or coconut.

Spread tops of cakes with marmalade and decorate with a puff of ready-whipped topping.

Spread tops of cakes with marshmallow topping; sprinkle with chocolate bits or grate a little bittersweet chocolate over each cake.

Top cakes with spoonfuls of sundae sauces, then with a little marshmallow topping.

Top cakes with marshmallow topping and place under medium broiler heat for a few seconds, to brown.

CUPCAKES, BIRTHDAY PARTY STYLE

Hint

Cut very hard brick ice cream into half-inch slices. Dip a biscuit cutter (slightly larger in diameter than the base of the cupcakes) into very hot water; press cutter down on center of ice cream slice to make a hole. Lift out center, and in the hole place a frosted cupcake. Put a birthday candle on each cake—but be sure to give Mr. Big a *special* cake—perhaps with colored frosting, or decorated with colored candy beads.

CHOCOLATE CHERRY CUPCAKES

6 un-iced bakery cupcakes
6 chocolate-covered "cordial" cherries

10 min.

Using a sharp pointed knife, cut a small scoop from tops of cakes. In each hole stand a cherry, bottom up. Place under low broiler heat for 2 or 3 minutes, or until chocolate melts; then spread chocolate over cake top.

Note: Chocolate will tend to hold its shape; poke

at it with a knife point to test; when chocolate is very soft, the cake is done.

Serves 6

INSTANT KING SIZE CUPCAKES

Time-saver

Turn sponge cake dessert shells over, so that the cup is on the bottom. Ice with any desired frosting.

Gingerbread

Bakery gingerbread makes a satisfying, tasty dessert after a light meal. The cake should always be served warmed, hence you can buy it a day in advance of when you'll want it. It will freshen while warming.

TO WARM GINGERBREAD (Or Any Pastry)

Time-saver

Pre-heat oven to moderate while you're preparing the meal. Just before you eat, turn oven off, and place gingerbread in oven. By the time you're through eating, it will be heated through, just warm enough.

BITTERSWEET GINGERBREAD

15 min.

- 1 bakery gingerbread, or 4 3-inch squares
- 1 square baking chocolate
- 2 tablespoons milk
- 1 cup canned chocolate sauce
- ⅛ teaspoon vanilla extract
- ½ cup heavy cream
- 1 teaspoon sugar
- ¼ teaspoon vanilla extract
- crystallized ginger

Place gingerbread in oven to freshen (if in cut squares, wrap in aluminum foil). Melt chocolate over hot water with milk, stir smooth; add chocolate sauce, 1/8 teaspoon vanilla extract and mix; keep over hot water. While chocolate is melting, whip cream very stiff, adding sugar and 1/4 teaspoon vanilla extract. To serve: cut gingerbread loaf into 3-inch squares; split squares. Spoon chocolate sauce on bottom halves, replace tops, spoon more sauce over. At the last moment before serving, top with whipped cream. Sprinkle a little finely chopped crystallized ginger over the whipped cream.

Serves 4

CREAM CHEESE GINGERBREAD

10 min.

- 1 3-oz. package cream cheese
- 2 tablespoons light cream
- 1 drop lemon extract
- 1 tablespoon sifted confectioner's sugar
- 1/2 cup finely chopped nuts
- 1 gingerbread (cake or loaf)

Warm gingerbread in a moderate oven (see Timesaver above). Soften cheese by combining with cream. Add all other ingredients and mix well. Spread on thin slices of gingerbread.

Serves 6

SPICE-ICED GINGERBREAD

15 min.

- 1 gingerbread (cake or loaf)
- 1 3-oz. package cream cheese
- 2 tablespoons heavy cream
- 1 cup confectioner's sugar
- 1/4 teaspoon cinnamon
- a pinch each of cloves, nutmeg and ginger
- ready-whipped topping
- chopped nuts
- cinnamon

If using a gingerbread cake, cut in half, and slice halves across to make 4 layers. If using a gingerbread loaf, cut loaf the long way into 4 layers. Thin cheese with cream, add sugar, the 1/4 teaspoon cinnamon and other spices. Mix until well combined and smooth. Spread each layer with cheese mixture and put together to make a 4-layer cake. Decorate top with a few swirls of ready-whipped topping and a few sprinkles of chopped nuts. Now fill a chilled serving bowl with ready-whipped topping and sprinkle very lightly with cinnamon. To serve: have bowl of whipped topping on the side. Cut cake into half-inch slices and garnish each portion with a generous spoonful of topping.

Serves 6 to 8

TIMESAVER VARIATION SPICE-ICED GINGERBREAD—

Make a double recipe of Coffeecake Frosting (see Index), adding 1 tablespoon or slightly more prepared mincemeat. Spread frosting over top of gingerbread loaf. Top with ready-whipped topping, or serve topping on the side, as above.

8 min.

APPLE BUTTER TOPPING FOR GINGERBREAD

Prepare apple butter and whipped cream combination as directed in recipe for Apple Butter Cake (see Index). Pile topping on a fresh, cool gingerbread.

Hint

Timesaver: Cover a cool gingerbread with ready-whipped topping; make hollows in topping with the back of a spoon, and drop a spoonful of apple butter into each hollow.

Hint

FANCY SUGAR DRESS FOR CAKE

Use an ordinary open-work paper doily, about as big around as the cake (or gingerbread); or, if the cake is square, use a larger doily and snip off the sides so that it just covers the surface of the cake. Place doily on cake; sprinkle over generously with sifted confectioner's sugar. Lift doily off carefully, and you'll have a handsome design!

8 min.

APRICOT GINGERBREAD

1 very hard pint tray-pack brick of peach ice cream
half a fresh, cool gingerbread
apricot halves, well drained
ready-whipped topping

Remove wrapping from ice cream and place brick on a sheet of waxed paper. Starting at end of the brick top farthest from you, dig a silver serving spoon about ½ inch into the surface. Draw spoon towards you, scraping off ice cream "curls." Cover top of cake with "curls," then nicely arrange apricot halves on ice cream. Garnish with puffs of ready-whipped topping.

Serves 4 to 6

Frostings

Frosting should be rich, but not *too* sweet, nor should the taste overpower the delicate flavor of the cake. Try also to have the frosting flavor complement the cake flavor. For example, use mocha frosting on a spice cake, or chocolate frosting on a white cake. (If your grocer sells chocolate layers, try using Bittersweet Frosting (see below).

SPREAD YOUR FROSTING HIGH, WIDE, AND HANDSOME

Hint

When icing a cake, don't just spread it over the cake in a neat, flat layer. Finish it off in swirls or peaks using the flat of a silver knife or the back of a spoon bowl. Your cake *looks* higher, and somehow, the swirls make it *taste* better!

QUICK CHOCOLATE FROSTING—BASIC RECIPE

5 min.

For One Cake Layer	*For Two Cake Layers*
1 package of a chocolate-flavored instant frosting mix	2 packages of a chocolate-flavored instant frosting mix
2 tablespoons sifted cocoa	¼ cup sifted cocoa
a tiny pinch of nutmeg	⅛ teaspoon scant, nutmeg
⅛ teaspoon vanilla extract	¼ teaspoon vanilla extract

(Use heavy cream for liquid, amount as directed on package.)

Measure required amount of cream into a cup, place cup in pan of water over high heat. When water boils, remove from heat. Meanwhile, turn frosting mix into bowl, add cocoa, and nutmeg; stir to mix. Measure vanilla into cream and finish frosting as directed on package.

Note: For extra rich quick frosting, after the first addition of liquid, beat in one egg yolk for each package of mix, using a rotary beater. Count yolk as one tablespoon of liquid; omit that much liquid from recipe.

One 6-oz. package of mix frosts one 8-inch cake layer or 8 to 12 cupcakes

QUICK CHOCOLATE FROSTING—VARIATIONS

CHOCOLATE MALT: For each package of mix add 1 tablespoon plain malted milk to recipe. Or omit 2 tablespoons cocoa and add 3 tablespoons chocolate malted milk mix.

BITTERSWEET: For each package of mix add 1 or 2 additional tablespoons sifted cocoa.

MOCHA: For each package of mix replace 2 teaspoons of cream with 2 teaspoons boiling water in which ½ teaspoon soluble coffee has been dissolved.

NUT: For each package of mix stir ½ cup or more chopped nuts into finished frosting.

5 min.

QUICK VANILLA FROSTING—BASIC RECIPE

For One Cake Layer	*For Two Cake Layers*
1 package of a vanilla-flavored instant frosting mix	2 packages of a vanilla-flavored instant frosting mix
2 tablespoons powdered malted milk	¼ cup powdered malted milk
⅛ teaspoon vanilla extract	¼ teaspoon vanilla extract
1 drop lemon extract	2 drops lemon extract

(Use heavy cream for liquid, amount as directed on package.)

Measure required amount of cream into a cup, place cup in pan of water over high heat. When water boils, remove from heat. Meanwhile, turn frosting mix into bowl, add malted milk and mix. Measure flavoring extracts into cream and finish frosting as directed on package.

Note: For extra rich quick frosting, see Note in Quick Chocolate Frosting, above.

One 6-oz. package of mix frosts one 8-inch layer cake or 8 to 12 cupcakes

QUICK VANILLA FROSTING—VARIATIONS

CHOCOLATE FROSTING MADE FROM VANILLA MIX: For each package of mix omit 1 tablespoon malted milk; add 3 tablespoons sifted cocoa and a tiny pinch of nutmeg. An extra teaspoon or so of cream may be required.

MOCHA VANILLA: For each package of mix replace 2 teaspoons cream with 2 teaspoons boiling water, in which ½ teaspoon of soluble coffee has been dissolved.

MOCHA RUM: For each package of mix replace 1 teaspoon of cream with 1 teaspoon of boiling water in which ½ teaspoon soluble coffee has been dissolved; replace vanilla extract with rum extract. Taste finished frosting; stir in more rum extract, if desired.

RUM: For each package of mix replace vanilla extract with rum extract. Taste finished frosting; add more flavor, if desired.

NUT: For each package of mix stir ½ cup or more chopped nuts into frosting.

BLACK WALNUT: For each package of mix replace lemon extract with one drop black walnut extract. Taste finished frosting and add more flavor, if desired. Stir in ½ cup chopped black or English walnuts.

SPICE: For each package of mix add ¼ teaspoon cinnamon, ⅛ teaspoon nutmeg and a tiny pinch each of cloves and ginger. Stir spices through dry mix before adding liquid. If desired, add a drop or two of rum extract.

PEPPERMINT: For each package of mix add one drop peppermint extract. Taste finished frosting; add more flavor, if desired.

ORANGE: For each package of mix replace 2 teaspoons cream with 2 teaspoons frozen concentrated orange juice, thawed to room temperature. Or, replace one tablespoon cream with one tablespoon orange juice. Add cream to frosting mix first; mix, then add orange juice. Add chopped candied orange peel, or fruitcake orange peel, if desired.

LEMON: For each package of mix replace 1 teaspoon cream with 1 teaspoon lemon juice. Add cream to frosting mix first; mix, then add fruit juice.

CHERRY: For each package of mix replace vanilla extract with cherry extract; lemon extract with almond. Add chopped maraschino or candied cherries, if desired, and a little red food coloring.

COCONUT: For each package of mix omit lemon extract; add 1 drop almond extract. Add from ¼ to ½ cup moist shredded coconut to finished frosting and mix well.

Time-saver

TO COCONUT THE SIDES OF A CAKE

Pick up a "bundle" of the coconut shreds between your thumb and index finger. Dab coconut at the sides of cake and it will stick.

15 min.

QUICK FROSTING WITH COCOA MIX

4 tablespoons hot cream
2½ cups sifted confectioner's sugar
3 tablespoons soft butter
¾ cup instant cocoa mix
¼ teaspoon vanilla extract
a tiny pinch of nutmeg

Measure cream into cup, place in a pan of water over high heat; when water boils, remove from heat. Measure about ½ cup sugar into mixing bowl, add butter, and cream until smooth. Add cocoa mix and cocoa. Cream again. Add 1 tablespoon cream and vanilla extract, stir until smooth; add remaining sugar and cream alternately, until frosting is of desired consistency.

Note: If cocoa mix is sweet-type, add 2 teaspoons sifted unsweetened cocoa. If desired, add 1 egg yolk after first addition of cream; omit 1 tablespoon cream.

Generously frosts 2 8-inch layers or 24 to 36 cupcakes

HOW TO DECORATE A CAKE

Hint

Smooth top of iced cake with a knife. Use a toothpick as a stylus and trace the name or design you want on the cake. If you make a slip, smooth icing over and correct. Then follow your tracing with frosting squeezed from a pastry tube.

If you haven't a pastry tube, roll a long cone from heavy waxed paper. Stick the seam closed with cellophane tape. Tear off tip of cone to make an opening not more than ¼ inch across, less if possible. Spoon frosting into cone; fold top over several times and clip shut with a paper clip. Squeeze cone gently to force out frosting.

HOW TO CUT A FROSTED CAKE

Hint

For butter- or cream-type frostings, run very hot water over a sharp knife, wipe dry, and cut. If icing sticks, reheat knife.

For fragile cakes, or cakes frosted with marshmallow-type frostings, cut first slice with a knife, then use two long-tined forks to "pull" off additional portions.

HOW TO TINT CAKE FROSTING

Hint

Use liquid food coloring (the kind available in sets of green, blue, yellow, and red). Package directions tell you how to make various colors.

To tint a small quantity of frosting for decorations, reserve three or four tablespoons of the finished batch, or as much as will be required. Add color, beat until evenly tinted. If desired, thin frosting slightly with a few drops of cream; decorations are easier to shape when frosting is slightly loose.

FROSTING FOR COFFEECAKE OR RAISIN BREAD

5 min.

1 tablespoon butter
½ cup sifted confectioner's sugar
pinch of salt
¼ teaspoon vanilla extract
2 or 3 teaspoons hot water

Cream butter, sugar, and salt together; add extract and enough hot water to make a thin paste. Apply frosting with a pastry brush, or, to make those fancy designs the bakeries tempt you with, let the frosting drip onto the pastry from the end of a tablespoon—moving the spoon to and fro to make a crisscross pattern.

Note: For an interesting variation, stir 1 tablespoon or slightly more prepared mincemeat into finished frosting.

For one large coffee cake or 4 to 6 pastries

Pies

Bakery pies plus a little ingenuity will give you good-tasting, good-looking "different" desserts for 20-Minute Cookery.

Keep bakery pies wrapped securely in waxed paper. Prepare only as many portions as you'll need for the meal; save the rest for next day. Keep cream pies under constant refrigeration, since cream fillings spoil easily.

HOW TO MAKE PERFECT WHIPPED CREAM EVERY TIME

7 min.

(For Topping Pies, Puddings, or other Desserts)

- ½ pint heavy cream, well chilled
- 2 teaspoons sugar
- ½ teaspoon vanilla extract

Add 2 drops almond extract for *custard* pies or desserts.
Add 1 drop lemon extract for *cream* pies or desserts.
Add 1 drop rum or brandy extract for *fruit* pies or desserts or match extract to pie filling (e.g. cherry extract to cherry pie).

If cream is not cold, turn it into an ice cube tray and place in freezing compartment of refrigerator for a few minutes. Do not allow cream to freeze. Rinse mixing bowl well with very cold water and dry. Whip cream with rotary beater until quite foamy, add sugar, vanilla, and other extract. Beat until cream is stiff enough to hold a well-defined peak, if used for toppings. If cream is to be folded into other mixtures, beat until very stiff—until it "resists" the beater. At this point cream is ready to churn into butter—beat slowly and carefully.

For topping an 8 or 9 inch pie or 6 to 8 portions dessert

HOW TO FLAVOR READY-WHIPPED TOPPINGS

Hint

Pipe about ½ cup ready-whipped topping into a measuring cup, rinsed well with cold water and dried. Add drops of flavoring extracts (omitting vanilla extract) as suggested in Whipped Cream (see above). Stir topping and extract gently to mix. Cover cool pie or dessert with a thin layer of flavored topping, then add more topping from container, as much as desired.

Note: Ready-whipped topping should not be used on hot or even *very* warm pastry; it will "melt." Use stiffly whipped cream instead and be sure pastry is only warm (not hot).

CREAM-FILLED DOUBLE-CRUST FRUIT PIES

5 min.

If you can get double-crust fruit pies with high, peaked crusts, do this: using a sharp, slim knife, bore 8 small holes around the crust, spacing intervals evenly. Into each hole in turn, insert the tip of a ready-whipped topping container and fill pie with cream. Garnish top with a puff or two of cream, if it's necessary to hide your trickery.

Note: Pie should not be heated. Store leftover pie in refrigerator.

DOUBLE-CRUST FRUIT PIES, FARM STYLE

14 min.

Brush top crust very, very lightly with melted butter; sprinkle with cinnamon sugar. Place pie in a medium oven 5 to 10 minutes, or until heated through.

CHEESE'N PIE

5 min.

Do this with mincemeat or apple pie. Cut into serving portions. Cut and trim cheese slices to same shape but slightly smaller than pie wedges. Slip a thin spatula under top crust and bend it back just enough to slip cheese wedge in. Best if pie is warmed.

PIE, DEEP-DISH STYLE

12 to 15 min.

Best with double-crust apple pies, but other fruit pies, single or double-crust, may be used. Heat pie through in a medium oven. Cut portions in squares, or in generous squat wedges and place in deep dessert dishes. Pour ¼ cup or more light cream over each portion and sprinkle very lightly with cinnamon sugar.

HIGH-HAT PIE

8 min.

Use a double-crust fruit pie, preferably with a flattish top. With a sharp knife point, cut neatly all around the top crust, just inside rim of pie. (Be careful not to pierce the bottom crust.) Now cut top crust into serving portions; slip a thin spatula under each crust wedge and remove to a sheet of waxed paper. Pile ready-whipped topping or stiffly whipped cream on pie in a thick, even layer. Replace top-crust wedges; pat lightly to "set" them in place. When serving pie, cut through divisions in top crust.

NOW YOU CAN EAT THE "BOTTOM CRUST"

(For Double-Crust Pies)

6 min.

If pie is not already packed in a paper "pan," slip it into a pie tin. Place a serving plate face down on top of pie. Pick up pie "pan" and plate together and turn over with a quick twist of your wrists. The top (and flaky) crust will now be the bottom crust. Remove pie pan carefully. (If it seems to stick, grasp pan rim at opposite sides and twist gently to loosen.) With a sharp pointed knife make one-inch cuts all around the edge of the new "top" crust; slip a thin spatula under it and remove. Fill top of pie with ready-whipped topping.

BERRY PIES WITH ICE CREAM

8 min.

Use single-crust pies. Gently scoop out filling and set aside. On bottom crust spread a layer of hard vanilla ice cream; return filling to pie and spread evenly. Decorate with ready-whipped topping.

FRUIT TURNOVERS

Hint

If made with thin "crusty" pastry, turnovers can also be filled with ready-whipped topping as directed in Cream-Filled Double-Crust Fruit Pies (above). Bore one or two holes in the top of each turnover.

HOW TO SERVE FRUIT PIE LEFTOVERS

Hint

Heat pie and cut into coarse chunks; heap up in serving dishes and serve as a pudding, with cream on the side. Cream may be flavored, if desired, as in Whipped Cream (see above).

Cooked-Pudding Desserts

VANILLA PUDDING

10 min.

milk for liquid
1 package vanilla pudding mix
few grains of salt
2 drops lemon extract
1 drop almond extract
2 teaspoons butter

Measure liquid into saucepan (see package for quantity), add pudding mix and salt; beat lightly to mix. Cook as directed on package. After removing from heat add flavoring extracts and butter; beat briskly with a rotary beater. Pudding is ready when slightly cooled.

Serves 4 to 6

CHOCOLATE PUDDING

10 min.

milk for liquid
1 package chocolate pudding mix
⅛ teaspoon salt
1 square baking chocolate (1 oz.)
2 teaspoons butter
½ teaspoon vanilla extract
a pinch of nutmeg

Measure liquid into saucepan (see package for quantity), add pudding mix and salt; beat lightly to mix. Add chocolate (unmelted) and cook as directed on package. After removing from heat add butter, vanilla extract and nutmeg; beat briskly with a rotary beater. Pudding is ready when slightlv cooled.

Serves 4 to 6

BUTTERSCOTCH PUDDING

10 min.

1 package butterscotch pudding mix
milk for liquid
few grains of salt
2 teaspoons butter
¼ teaspoon maple flavoring
2 drops brandy extract

Measure liquid into a saucepan (see package for quantity), add pudding mix and salt; beat lightly to mix. Cook as directed on package. After removing from heat add butter and flavoring, beat briskly with a rotary beater. Pudding is ready when slightly cooled.

Serves 4 to 6

TO COOL PUDDING QUICKLY

Time-saver

Pour hot pudding into a cake pan; spread evenly; press aluminum foil or waxed paper onto surface of pudding to prevent film. Place on a cake rack, or, for even quicker cooling, place cake pan in refrigerator (but not under ice cube compartment). Pudding cools in a few minutes. Before serving, stir well.

TAPIOCA PUDDING

milk for liquid
1 egg yolk
few grains of salt
1 package tapioca pudding mix
2 teaspoons butter
¼ teaspoon vanilla extract

10 min.

Measure liquid into a saucepan (see package for quantity), add egg yolk and salt and beat lightly. Add pudding mix and mix well. Cook as directed on package. After removing from heat add butter and vanilla extract; beat briskly with a rotary beater. Pudding is ready when slightly cooled.

Serves 4 to 6

RICE PUDDING

10 min.

- milk for liquid
- 1 egg yolk
- few grains of salt
- 1 package rice pudding mix
- ¼ cup raisins
- 2 teaspoons butter
- ⅛ teaspoon cinnamon
- ¼ teaspoon vanilla extract

Measure liquid into a saucepan (see package for quantity), add egg yolk and salt and beat lightly. Add pudding mix and raisins and mix well. Cook as directed on package. After removing from heat, add butter, cinnamon and vanilla extract; beat with a spoon. Cool slightly before serving.

Serves 4 to 6

PUDDING HOT OR PUDDING COLD?

Hint

Most packaged pudding instructions direct you to chill the pudding before serving. Use your own taste sense—serve puddings warm, or even hot, if you desire. There's no set rule you must follow—except that a pudding should have a rich, satisfying flavor.

COCONUT-CREAM PUDDING

- milk for liquid
- 1 egg yolk
- few grains of salt
- 1 package coconut-cream pudding mix
- 2 teaspoons butter
- ¼ teaspoon vanilla extract
- ¼ to ½ cup moist shredded coconut

10 min.

Measure liquid into saucepan (see package for quantity), add egg yolk and salt and beat lightly. Add pudding mix and mix well. Cook as directed on package. After removing from heat add butter and vanilla extract; beat with a rotary beater. Stir in coconut. Cool slightly before serving.

Serves 4 to 6

15 min.

COCONUT-BREAD PUDDING

Prepare Coconut-Cream Pudding as directed above, omitting coconut; to uncooked pudding add ¼ cup raisins, ⅛ teaspoon nutmeg and a generous pinch of cinnamon. Just before serving, stir in 2 or 3 slices of crisply toasted raisin bread, well buttered and diced.

10 min.

LEMON PUDDING

1 package lemon-pie-filling mix
1 egg yolk
1 tablespoon butter
2 or 3 drops lemon extract

Prepare pudding as directed on package, adding the 1 extra egg yolk. After removing from heat, stir in butter and extract.

Note: Lemon pudding makes a tasty and refreshing dessert after a hearty meal.

Serves 4 to 6

12 min.

MOCHA CREAM PUDDING

1 recipe Vanilla Pudding (see Index)
½ teaspoon soluble coffee
2 tablespoons boiling water

or

1 recipe Butterscotch Pudding (see Index)
⅓ teaspoon soluble coffee
2 tablespoons boiling water

Prepare pudding as directed, adding to milk the soluble coffee dissolved in boiling water.

Serves 4 to 6

Time-saver

COOK PUDDINGS THIS "NO-WATCH" WAY

If you have other cooking which needs your attention, make your pudding dessert this way and you won't be tied to the stove, stirring and watching.

Start 2 cups water boiling in double boiler bottom, over highest heat. Measure pudding ingredients into double boiler top; mix thoroughly. Cook, covered, over gently boiling water for up to 30 minutes; just give pudding a frequent stirring. When ready to finish pudding, stir briskly, then beat with a rotary beater. Place over direct heat and cook as directed on package. It will take only a minute or two.

VANILLA MINT PUDDING

12 min.

- 1 recipe Vanilla Pudding (see Index)
- 6 to 10 miniature chocolate-covered cream-center mints

Prepare pudding as directed. After removing from heat and stirring in flavorings, add mints, cut in halves. Stir pudding gently, just enough to swirl streaks of chocolate through the pudding. Larger mint patties may be used if cut into small bits.

Serves 4 to 6

CHOCOLATE MINT PUDDING

12 min.

Prepare Chocolate Pudding (see Index) as directed, omitting baking chocolate. When flavored, add 6 to 10 chocolate mints (see above).

FLAVORING MAGIC BY THE DROP

Time-saver

Nothing adds flavor to desserts more quickly or easily than flavoring extracts. There are many varieties besides the traditional vanilla: almond, lemon, orange, black-walnut, rum, brandy, cherry — and more. Just remember that these extracts are potent; add flavoring in *drops,* and taste as you go. It's easy to overflavor.

If you use vanilla extract frequently, buy the large size and save money. Buy small sizes of other flavors you may not use so often. Keep extracts on a cool shelf; always tighten bottle caps securely.

Select good brands of extracts. If you have a choice between an "imitation flavor" and a "pure extract," always buy the "pure." It costs more, but it has more flavoring power.

CHOCOLATE ROLLS

- 1 recipe Chocolate Pudding (see Index)
- 1 or 2 ladyfingers per serving
- ½ cup heavy cream
- 1 teaspoon sugar
- ¼ teaspoon vanilla extract
- ½ cup semi-sweet chocolate, shaved

20 min.

When pudding is ready, cool as directed in To Cool Pudding Quickly (see Timesaver Index). Meanwhile split ladyfingers; whip cream very stiff adding sugar and vanilla extract. Make thick sandwiches by coating ladyfinger-halves with pudding; also spoon pudding over tops. Just before serving, top each roll with whipped cream and sprinkle on shaved chocolate.

Timesaver: Use ready-whipped topping instead of whipped cream; use "chocolate sprinkles" (cake decorations) instead of shaved chocolate.

Makes 6 to 8

CHOCOLATE ROLLS—VARIATIONS

20 min.

LEMON: Use Lemon Pudding (see Index). Sprinkle tops of finished rolls with a little finely chopped candied orange or lemon peel. If topped with your own-make whipped cream add 1 drop lemon extract.

BUTTERSCOTCH: Use Butterscotch Pudding or Mocha Cream Pudding made with Butterscotch Pudding (see Index). Sprinkle tops of finished rolls with chopped toasted almonds.

VANILLA: Use Vanilla Pudding (see Index). Spread each ladyfinger-half lightly with canned chocolate syrup before spreading with pudding; sprinkle top of finished pudding with shaved chocolate as directed.

BANANA: Use Vanilla Pudding (see Index). Spread each ladyfinger-half lightly with pudding, then cover with sliced bananas. Spoon more pudding over bananas; finish rolls as directed. Garnish top with a few banana slices.

TAPIOCA PLUM PUDDING

15 min.

- 1 recipe Tapioca Pudding (see Index)
- about 6 canned plums, well drained
- tiny pinch each of salt and nutmeg
- whipped cream
- cinnamon sugar

Prepare pudding as directed. Meanwhile, pit and quarter plums. Cool cooked pudding slightly, first stirring in nutmeg and salt. Fold in fruit. Serve topped with whipped cream, sprinkle lightly with cinnamon sugar.

Serves 4 to 6

TAPIOCA PLUM PUDDING—VARIATIONS

15 min.

With Vanilla, Tapioca, or Rice Pudding (see Index) use well-drained frozen or canned peaches; frozen or canned strawberries, raspberries, loganberries or cherries (do not use sour pie cherries); chopped dates or figs; canned pineapple; cooked rhubarb.

With Lemon Pudding (see Index) use well-drained frozen or canned peaches; canned plums, pineapple, grapefruit, orange segments or cherries (do not use sour pie cherries); stewed prunes or apricots; or prunes and apricots combined.

15 min.

BERRY PUDDING

- 1 #2 can raspberries, strawberries, or loganberries
- milk
- 1 package vanilla pudding mix
- few grains of salt
- 2 teaspoons butter
- 2 drops almond extract
- 1 drop lemon extract
- heavy cream

Drain syrup from berries into a measuring cup, add milk to make quantity of liquid called for on package and pour into a saucepan. Add pudding mix and salt; mix. Cook as directed on package. After removing from heat add butter and flavoring extracts; beat briskly with a rotary beater. Cool pudding slightly and carefully fold in fruit without crushing. Serve with unsweetened cream on the side.

Serves 4 to 6

15 min.

BERRY PUDDING—VARIATIONS

Use Vanilla or Coconut-Cream Pudding (see Index). Prepare liquid called for in pudding recipe by draining into a measuring cup syrup from one of the following: frozen or canned sliced peaches, canned fruit cocktail, canned pears (diced), frozen or canned cherries (do not use sour pie cherries). To syrup add ½ teaspoon lemon juice and mix well. Add milk to make quantity of liquid called for on pudding-mix package, and cook as directed. Fold in fruit as directed.

12 min.

FIG PUDDING

- 1 recipe Vanilla Pudding (see Index)
- 1 16-oz. can fig pudding or 6 or 8 canned figs
- heavy cream

Prepare pudding as directed. After adding flavorings, add canned fig pudding, diced or coarsely chopped well-drained canned figs. Stir lightly and serve at once, with unsweetened cream on the side.

Note: Date and nut bread, leftover plum pudding, or fruitcake may be substituted for canned fig pudding.

Serves 4 to 6

CHOCOLATE MERINGUES

half-recipe Chocolate Pudding (see Index)
2 egg whites
2 tablespoons granulated sugar
4 sponge cake shortcake cups

20 min.

Start oven pre-heating to 400°. Prepare pudding and cool slightly (see Timesaver Index, To Cool Pudding Quickly). Beat egg whites until foamy, using a rotary beater, add sugar and beat until stiff but not dry. Fill cake cups with pudding; pile with meringue, covering edge of cake. Arrange cakes in a pie tin inside another pan containing a little hot water; place in oven 5 to 8 minutes or until lightly browned.

Serves 4

MERINGUES—VARIATIONS, USING LEFTOVER CAKE

20 min.

Cut half-inch slices of cake into squares or rectangles; remove icing.

With *white cake* use Vanilla, Butterscotch, Lemon, or Tapioca Pudding.

With *chocolate cake* use Vanilla, Mocha Cream, or Chocolate Pudding.

With *spice cake* use Butterscotch, Lemon, or Mocha Cream Pudding.

See Index for pudding recipes; use ½ recipe for four servings.

20 min.

CHOCOLATE PUDDING SURPRISE

1 recipe Chocolate Pudding (see Index)
1 pint brick vanilla ice cream
ready-whipped topping

Prepare pudding as directed and cool to room temperature (see Timesaver Index, How to Cool Pudding Quickly). Just before time to serve, turn pudding into a bowl, whisk lightly with a fork. Add ice cream, cut into 1 inch cubes. Fold together lightly. Serve at once, garnished with puffs of ready-whipped topping.

Serves 6 to 8

20 min.

CHOCOLATE PUDDING SURPRISE—VARIATIONS

With Vanilla Pudding use chocolate, cherry, or strawberry ice cream.

With Butterscotch Pudding use maple-nut, butter-pecan, or toasted almond ice cream.

With Lemon Pudding use vanilla ice cream.

With Tapioca Pudding or Rice Pudding use vanilla, strawberry, cherry, or coffee ice cream.

See Index for pudding recipes.

ICE CREAM PUDDING SANDWICHES

1 recipe pudding mix
ice cream
ready-whipped topping

20 min.

For flavor combinations see Chocolate Pudding Surprise and Variations, above. Spread a half-inch slice of ice cream with cooled pudding (see Timesaver Index, How To Cool Pudding Quickly). Top with another slice of ice cream; garnish with a spoonful of pudding and puffs of ready-whipped topping.

Serves 6 to 8

Quick Uncooked-Pudding Desserts

Hints

For best results with quick uncooked pudding mixes have liquid ingredients very cold. If not, chill this way: place several ice cubes in a bowl, add liquid, stir until ice cold. Or turn liquid into an ice cube tray and place in freezing compartment of your refrigerator. It will chill in about 15 minutes.

When chilling milk with ice cubes, as directed above, use ¾ milk and ¼ light cream to retain richness (melting ice will dilute plain milk).

To enrich uncooked puddings use half milk and half cream for liquid, or beat two egg yolks or one whole egg into milk. (Count egg as part of liquid. Break egg into measuring cup and add milk to make required amount of liquid.)

EGG NOG PUDDING

5 min.

2 eggs
⅛ teaspoon salt
¼ teaspoon brandy extract
pinch of nutmeg
milk for liquid
1 package vanilla instant pudding mix

Break eggs into measuring cup, add salt, extract, and nutmeg; add milk to make quantity of liquid called for on package and beat with a rotary beater until well combined. Finish pudding as directed on package. Serve topped with ready-whipped topping over which a few grains of nutmeg have been sprinkled.

Serves 4 to 6

4 min.

PINEAPPLE PUDDING

1 9-oz. can pineapple tidbits
lemon juice, if needed
pineapple juice
milk for liquid
1 drop lemon extract
1 package vanilla instant pudding mix
ready-whipped topping

Drain syrup from pineapple into a measuring cup; if very sweet add up to 1 teaspoon lemon juice. Add pineapple juice to make 1 cup; add milk to make quantity of liquid called for on package. Add lemon extract and combine liquid. Complete pudding as directed on package. To serve: Turn into sherbet glasses, stick pineapple tidbits around edge of glasses and fill center with topping.

Serves 4 to 6

SIX-MINUTE PRUNE WHIP

1 8-oz. jar "junior" chopped prunes
½ teaspoon lemon juice
milk for liquid
⅛ teaspoon cinnamon
1 package vanilla instant pudding mix
½ cup heavy cream
1 teaspoon sugar
¼ teaspoon vanilla extract
1 drop lemon extract

6 min.

Combine prunes, lemon juice, and milk to make quantity of liquid called for on pudding package. Stir cinnamon through dry mix, add milk, and beat vigorously until stiff and smooth, using a rotary beater. Whip cream stiff, adding sugar, vanilla and lemon extracts. Fold into pudding until just barely combined.

Serves 4 to 6

FRUIT NECTAR PUDDING

1 cup apricot, peach, or pear nectar
1 teaspoon lemon juice
2 drops lemon extract
tiny pinch of salt
milk for liquid
1 package vanilla instant pudding mix

Pour nectar into a measuring cup, add lemon juice, extract, and salt; mix. Add milk to make quantity of liquid called for on pudding package. Follow package directions to finish pudding.

4 min.

Serves 4 to 6

MALTED MILK PUDDING

1 package vanilla instant pudding mix and 1 to 2 tablespoons plain malted milk **or** 1 package chocolate instant pudding mix and 1 to 2 tablespoons chocolate malted milk
milk for liquid

Turn pudding mix into a bowl, add malted milk. Stir thoroughly to combine. Add milk (see package for amount of liquid). Finish pudding as directed on package.

4 min.

Serves 4 to 6

MELON BALL PUDDING

1 recipe Spiced Melon Balls (see Index)
1 recipe Fruit Nectar Pudding (above)
ready-whipped topping

Prepare melon balls as directed. While melon is chilling, prepare pudding. To serve: spoon a thin layer of pudding into sherbet glasses; place melon balls around edge. Fill center with pudding; top with ready-whipped topping.

20 min.

Serves 4 to 6

4 min.

APPLE BUTTER PUDDING

½ cup apple butter
a pinch of salt
milk for liquid
1 package vanilla instant pudding mix
4 graham crackers, crumbled
1 package vanilla instant pudding mix

Turn apple butter into a measuring cup. Add salt, then milk to make quantity of liquid called for on pudding package. Mix well. Finish pudding as directed on package.

Serves 4 to 6

6 to 10 min.

CHEESE CAKE PUDDING

½ pint (1 cup) sour cream
milk for liquid
1 teaspoon vanilla extract
⅛ teaspoon salt
⅛ teaspoon cinnamon
1 package vanilla instant pudding mix
4 graham crackers, crumbled
cinnamon sugar
whipped cream or ready-whipped topping

Turn sour cream into a measuring cup; add milk to make quantity of liquid called for on package; add 2 additional tablespoons of milk, vanilla extract, and salt; beat well to combine. Stir cinnamon through dry mix, add milk mixture and beat with a rotary beater until stiff.

To serve:

I. Turn pudding into serving bowl, sprinkle top lightly with graham cracker crumbs, then with a little cinnamon sugar.

II. Turn pudding into serving bowl, spread with a layer of whipped cream or ready-whipped topping, over which lightly sprinkle graham cracker crumbs and cinnamon sugar.

III. For extra fancy service, butter very lightly the insides of sherbet glasses, pat fine graham cracker crumbs into place, then fill glasses with pudding. Top with whipped cream or ready-whipped topping, over which sprinkle a few more crumbs and cinnamon sugar.

Serves 4 to 6

QUICK CHOCOLATE PUDDING

4 min.

1 package vanilla instant pudding mix
2 tablespoons cocoa, sifted
milk for liquid
2 tablespoons chocolate syrup
½ teaspoon vanilla extract

Turn pudding mix into a bowl, add cocoa and stir through. Pour about 1 cup milk into a measuring cup, add chocolate syrup and extract. Mix well. Add milk to make quantity of liquid called for on package. Follow package directions to finish pudding.

Serves 4 to 6

QUICK MOCHA PUDDING

4 min.

½ teaspoon soluble coffee
1 tablespoon boiling water
milk for liquid
1 package vanilla or butterscotch instant pudding mix

Dissolve coffee in water and add to quantity of milk called for on package. Follow package directions to finish pudding.

Serves 4 to 6

4 min.

QUICK COCONUT PUDDING

1 drop almond extract
milk for liquid
½ cup or more moist shredded coconut
1 package vanilla instant pudding mix

Add extract to quantity of milk called for on package. Stir coconut through pudding mix before adding liquid; finish pudding as directed on package.

Serves 4 to 6

5 min.

QUICK SPICE PUDDING

1 egg or 2 egg yolks
¼ teaspoon cinnamon
⅛ teaspoon cloves
a tiny pinch each of nutmeg and ginger
milk for liquid
1 package butterscotch or vanilla instant pudding mix

Break egg into a measuring cup; add spices; add milk to make quantity of liquid called for on package. Beat liquid well. Follow package directions to finish pudding.

Serves 4 to 6

5 min.

QUICK RUM PUDDING

1 egg or 2 egg yolks
¼ to ½ teaspoon rum extract
milk for liquid
1 package vanilla instant pudding mix

Break egg into measuring cup; add extract; add milk to make quantity of liquid called for on package. Beat liquid well. Follow package directions to finish pudding.

Note: Brandy extract may be used instead of rum, if desired.

Serves 4 to 6

QUICK ORANGE PUDDING

5 min.

½ cup pear nectar
½ cup orange juice
milk for liquid
1 package vanilla instant pudding mix

Measure nectar and juice into a measuring cup, add milk to make quantity of liquid called for on package. Mix well. Follow package directions to finish pudding.

Serves 4 to 6

QUICK ORANGE PUDDING—VARIATION

GRAPEFRUIT: Use sweetened grapefruit juice instead of orange juice.

QUICK LEMON PUDDING

5 min.

½ cup pear nectar
1 tablespoon lemon juice
⅛ teaspoon lemon extract
milk for liquid
1 package vanilla instant pudding mix

Measure nectar and juice into a measuring cup, add lemon extract; mix well and add milk to make quantity of liquid called for on package. Follow package directions to finish pudding.

Serves 4 to 6

QUICK LEMON PUDDING—VARIATION

LIME: Use 5 teaspoons lime juice instead of lemon juice.

QUICK CHERRY PUDDING

up to 1 cup syrup from canned or frozen black, red, or white cherries (do not use sour pie cherries)
lemon juice, if needed
⅛ teaspoon cherry extract
1 drop almond extract
milk for liquid
1 package vanilla instant pudding mix
1 cup cherries or more

5 min.

Turn syrup into measuring cup. If very sweet, add up to 2 teaspoons lemon juice. Add flavoring extracts and mix well. Add milk to make quantity of liquid called for on package. Follow package directions to finish pudding. Serve pudding topped with cherries (or reserve fruit for another dessert).

Serves 4 to 6

Fruit

APPLESAUCE CREAM

10 min.

1 #2 can applesauce, chilled
1 tablespoon sugar
¼ teaspoon cinnamon
tiny pinch of salt
½ cup heavy cream
2 teaspoons sugar
¼ teaspoon vanilla extract
1 drop lemon extract
cinnamon sugar

Combine first 4 ingredients; beat with a rotary beater for a few moments and return to refrigerator. Whip cream very stiff, adding sugar and extracts. Just before serving fold applesauce and whipped cream together; sprinkle lightly with cinnamon sugar. Serve with cookies or thin slices of warm, un-iced cake or bake cupcakes (see Index).

Serves 6 to 8

CHEESE APPLESAUCE

8 min.

1 #2 can applesauce, chilled
1 tablespoon sugar
¼ teaspoon cinnamon
tiny pinch each of cloves and salt
4 or more slices Cheddar or Swiss cheese
ready-whipped topping

Turn applesauce, sugar, and spices into a bowl and beat with a rotary beater for a few moments. Cut cheese into half-inch squares (see Timesaver below) and fold into applesauce. Serve topped with puffs of ready-whipped topping.

Serves 6 to 8

TO DICE SLICED CHEESE QUICKLY

Time-saver

Lay slice of cheese on a sheet of waxed paper. Make even criss-cross cuts by pressing down with a sharp knife. The finer the cuts, the finer the dice. Pick up waxed paper and turn upside down over bowl; push cheese bits into bowl with fingers. Repeat for each slice.

PEAR INNOCENCE

5 min.

1 #2 can chilled pears
½ cup fruit cocktail
white crème de menthe

Drain syrup from pears. Reserve for another dish, except for a few teaspoons to be used in the bottom of each dessert saucer. For each portion arrange two pear-halves with cavities up, stems pointing in opposite directions. Garnish each portion with a few bits of fruit cocktail. In each pear cavity place a generous half-teaspoon crème de menthe.

Serves 4

MAPLE GRAPEFRUIT

5 min.

1 #2 can well-chilled grapefruit sections
¼ cup maple syrup
⅓ cup fruit cocktail
maple sugar

Drain ¼ cup syrup from grapefruit into a bowl; reserve remainder of syrup for another dish. Add maple syrup, then grapefruit. Mix. Serve in individual saucers garnished with fruit cocktail with a little maple sugar grated over each portion or have a bowl of grated maple sugar on the table.

Serves 4 to 6

"HOME STYLE" CANNED PEACHES

Hint

Your grocer probably carries a variety of canned peaches usually labeled "home style" or "old-fashioned style." If he doesn't, it's worth going out of your way to look for them. The peaches are packed in a slightly thinner, less sweet syrup, and lack just enough "polish" in their appearance to look like real home-canned peaches. What's more, they *taste* like home canning.

SPICED MELON BALLS

20 min.

- 1 well-ripened cantaloupe chilled
- 1 teaspoon lemon juice
- 2 tablespoons orange juice
- ⅛ teaspoon cinnamon
- ⅛ teaspoon ginger
- a tiny pinch of cloves
- ready-whipped topping

Cut melon in half, discard seeds; use a melon scoop to make balls. If melon is not chilled, place balls in an ice cube tray and put in freezing compartment of refrigerator; they will chill in 8 to 12 minutes. Meanwhile whisk other ingredients (except topping) together, using a fork. When melon is ready, turn into a deep bowl, pour juice mixture over and toss lightly. Serve in goblets, with a puff of ready-whipped topping on each portion.

Timesaver: Use frozen melon balls, thawed. (Call your grocer well ahead of time and ask him to remove the package from his freezer, so they'll be thawed when you pick them up.)

Serves 4 to 6

FRUIT CROUTONS

Hint

Slice day-old plain or sugar doughnuts into quarter-inch rings (like sliced frankfurters). Spread out in a cake pan and toast lightly under medium broiler heat (takes about 3 minutes). Sprinkle a few "croutons" on each portion of canned fruit .Two doughnuts make plenty for 4 portions.

STRAWBERRY PINEAPPLE CREAM

1 9-oz. can pineapple tidbits
port wine
1 #2 can strawberries or 1 package frozen sliced strawberries, thawed
½ cup heavy cream
1 teaspoon sugar
¼ teaspoon vanilla extract
1 drop lemon extract
maraschino cherries

10 min.

Drain syrup from pineapple and fill can with wine. Drain syrup from berries; reserve syrups for another dish. Whip cream very stiff, adding sugar and flavoring extracts. At the last moment before serving, drain wine from pineapple, turn fruit into a bowl, add strawberries. Toss lightly to combine. Fold in whipped cream. Pile into serving dishes; garnish with maraschino cherries.

Serves 4 to 6

KEEP CANNED FRUITS IN YOUR REFRIGERATOR

Time-saver

To be at its best fruit should be well chilled. Keep cans of your favorites in your refrigerator instead of on your shelf. They'll be ready-cold, any time you need them.

CANNED FRUIT COMBINATIONS

FRUIT AND NUT PEARS: Combine ¼ cup or slightly more fruit cocktail, well drained; a few tablespoons of chopped almonds and a tablespoon of cognac. Spoon a little of this over canned pears.

GINGER FRUIT: Sprinkle canned peaches, pears,

black or white cherries with chopped crystallized ginger. Canned fruitcake orange or lemon peels, chopped, may also be used.

BERRY PATCH APRICOTS: Drain canned raspberries, strawberries, or loganberries, and canned apricots; spoon berries over the apricots. Combine the syrups, add a teaspoon of lemon juice and pour a little syrup over the fruit. If desired, sprinkle confectioner's sugar over each portion at the last moment before serving.

LEMON-SWEET FRUIT: Spoon fruit from can into serving dish. Add a teaspoon or two of lemon juice to syrup in can; combine and taste; add more lemon juice until syrup is rather tart. Pour syrup over fruit.

LIQUEUR-FLAVORED FRUIT: Before you sit down to dinner, sprinkle a few tablespoons of cognac, kirsch, cointreau or other liqueur over drained canned raspberries or loganberries. Spoon berries over canned pears.

CRANBERRY FRUIT: Pile the cavities of canned peaches or pears with whole-berry canned cranberry sauce.

CRANBERRY FRUIT—VARIATION: Use a melon ball cutter to cut balls from cranberry jelly; turn a ball or two into the cavities of canned fruit.

MINCEMEAT FRUIT: Turn a teaspoon or two of ready-to-use mincemeat into the cavities of canned peaches or pears. If mincemeat is too tart, combine with a little sugar.

DRESS-UP FOR CANNED FRUIT: With any canned fruit, serve a bowl of plain crisp vanilla, sugar, or ginger cookies heated in the oven for a few moments.

TOPAZ FRUIT: Dice apple jelly (see below) and sprinkle the cubes over canned fruit. Especially good with pears.

HOW TO DICE JELLY

Hint

Use firm apple jelly. Open a fresh glass. Insert a thin knife blade between glass and jelly and go around to loosen jelly; turn out in one piece onto a large plate. Trim jelly into a cube, using a sharp knife; return trimmings to glass. Cut cube into slices, slices into bars, bars into dice. Lift dice with a spatula. Canned cranberry jelly may also be prepared this way.

Dessert Sauces

The 20-minute cook is often tempted to short-cut dessert preparation, only because there are so many *good* desserts available which need but little kitchen work to be tasty.

But food should not only *taste* good, it should *look* good. And that's where dessert sauces come in. They do double duty by adding more than goodness and flavor to the dessert; a dressing of sauce automatically describes you as a cook wise in the ways of food and its preparation.

So use dessert sauces often—to prepare them you'll need but few of your precious minutes and practically *none* of your energy. *Packaged puddings make the big difference!*

WHEN AND HOW TO SERVE DESSERT SAUCES

Use over hot or cold puddings; over warmed cake or pastry; over canned fruits; over ice cream.

Sauce should complement or contrast with the basic flavor of the dessert. For example, Jelly Sauce (see Index) is tart, and contrasts with a bland, sweet pudding; Bittersweet Chocolate Sauce (see Index) complements a chocolate pudding. When serving sauces over fruit, match the fruit and sauce flavors, or serve a sauce from the same family as the fruit itself.

Hints

Be careful not to "drown" the dessert flavor with too much sauce. It's best when used sparingly; serve a bowl of extra sauce for those who might want more. Don't cover the entire dessert with sauce; dribble it on with a spoon, or just make a swath of sauce across the surface.

Add interest and color to sauces by stirring in a little well-drained finely chopped fruit cocktail, chopped maraschino cherries, chopped nuts, shredded coconut, or chopped fruitcake fruit.

3 min.

COOKED-PUDDING DESSERT SAUCE

4 tablespoons leftover cooked pudding dessert
4 tablespoons cream or fruit juice

If film has formed on pudding, remove and discard. Measure pudding into a small bowl, add liquid; whisk with a fork until well blended and smooth. For thinner sauce, use slightly more liquid; for thicker sauce, reduce amount of liquid.

Timesaver: Four tablespoons of pudding won't be missed from a pudding dessert you might prepare; set it aside and use it as the "dress-up" for the next night's quick dessert.

Serves 4

3 to 5 min.

UNCOOKED-PUDDING SAUCE DESSERT—BASIC RECIPE

3 level tablespoons instant pudding mix
½ cup liquid

Measure pudding mix into a bowl. Add liquid and beat until smooth with a rotary beater. Makes a sauce of medium thickness; slightly more or less liquid may be used.

Note: For flavor of pudding and liquid ingredient see Variations, below.

Serves 4 to 6

UNCOOKED PUDDING SAUCES—VARIATIONS

BITTERSWEET CHOCOLATE: Use chocolate flavor mix. Stir 1 tablespoon sifted cocoa and a tiny pinch of nutmeg through dry mix. For liquid use ½ cup milk; add ¼ teaspoon vanilla extract.

Note: As little as 1 teaspoon cocoa may be used, if desired.

COFFEE: Use vanilla or butterscotch flavor mix; dissolve ¼ teaspoon soluble coffee in 1 tablespoon boiling water; add 2 tablespoons cream and enough milk to make ½ cup liquid.

RUM OR BRANDY: Use vanilla flavor mix; to 1 egg yolk add ¼ teaspoon brandy or rum extract. Add milk to make ½ cup liquid; beat well before adding to dry mix.

ORANGE: Use vanilla flavor mix. Add pear nectar to 1 tablespoon frozen orange juice concentrate to make ½ cup liquid. Add 2 drops orange extract and a tiny drop of almond extract. (Orange juice may be used instead of nectar-concentrate combination.)

LEMON: Use vanilla flavor mix. Add pear nectar to 1 tablespoon or less lemon juice to make ½ cup liquid; add 2 drops lemon extract and 1 tiny drop almond extract.

LIME: Use vanilla flavor mix. For liquid use sweetened lime juice (bottled) or add 3 tablespoons fresh lime juice to pear nectar to make ½ cup. Add 1 tiny drop almond extract.

GRAPEFRUIT: Use vanilla flavor mix. For liquid use sweetened grapefruit juice. Add 1 drop orange extract.

PINEAPPLE: Use vanilla flavor mix. For liquid use sweetened pineapple juice or ½ cup crushed pineapple plus ¼ cup pineapple juice. Add 1 drop lemon extract.

PINEAPPLE-COCONUT: Add ¼ cup moist shredded coconut to finished Pineapple Sauce above. Using a scissors or sharp knife, cut pineapple strands into small bits for a more attractive sauce.

JELLY SAUCE

3 min.

half a 10-oz. glass apple jelly
1 level tablespoon vanilla instant pudding mix

Turn jelly into a bowl; beat with a rotary beater until it looks like butterscotch. Stir pudding mix in with a spoon until well blended; beat with rotary beater until smooth.

Note: This sauce is especially good over warmed plain cake, coffeecake, with chopped nuts added or as an ice cream topping.

Serves 4 to 6

QUICK FRUIT SAUCE FOR CAKE

12 min.

1 #2 can plums
4 to 6 tablespoons sugar
¼ teaspoon lemon extract
1 drop almond extract
a tiny pinch of salt
5 teaspoons cornstarch

Combine, in a saucepan, syrup from plums and all other ingredients. If fruit has pits, remove; crush fruit lightly with a fork or cut in halves. Add to pan. Cook and stir over medium low heat until thick and clear. Serve over sponge cake layers or in sponge cake shortcake shells, warmed for a few minutes in the oven.

For two 8-inch layers

SUNDAE SAUCES

Hint

Some groceries or confectionery stores carry packaged ice-cream-sundae sauces. When you spot them, lay in a supply for when you're *really* short of time. Keep a can of chopped nuts and a jar of candied or maraschino cherries also ready; when you need a dessert that looks colorful and exciting, make your own ice cream sundaes. Top the sundaes with ready-whipped topping for the final touch.

Reminder: Your neighborhood soda fountain will always sell you enough fruit or nut topping so you can make sundaes at home.

Index of Recipes

Index of Hints and Timesavers